Accent on Orff

AN INTRODUCTORY APPROACH

Konnie K. Saliba
Memphis State University

PRENTICE HALL, Englewood Cliffs, New Jersey 07632

Library of Congress Cataloging-in-Publication Data

Saliba, Konnie K. (date)
  Accent on Orff : an introductory approach
 Konnie K. Saliba.
     p.   cm.
   Includes bibliographical references and index.
   ISBN 0-13-005208-6
   1. School music—Instruction and study. 2. Orff, Carl, 1895–
 Orff-Schulwerk.   I. Title.
 MT1.S235 1991
 372.87—dc20
                                                    90-41942
                                                       CIP
                                                       MN

Editorial/production supervision and
   interior design: Carole R. Crouse
Cover design: Diane Conner
Prepress buyer: Herb Klein
Manufacturing buyer: Dave Dickey

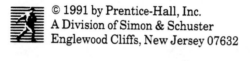 © 1991 by Prentice-Hall, Inc.
A Division of Simon & Schuster
Englewood Cliffs, New Jersey 07632

Printed in the United States of America

10 9 8 7 6 5 4 3 2 1

ISBN 0-13-005208-6

PRENTICE-HALL INTERNATIONAL (UK) LIMITED, *London*
PRENTICE-HALL OF AUSTRALIA PTY. LIMITED, *Sydney*
PRENTICE-HALL CANADA INC., *Toronto*
PRENTICE-HALL HISPANOAMERICANA, S.A., *Mexico*
PRENTICE-HALL OF INDIA PRIVATE LIMITED, *New Delhi*
PRENTICE-HALL OF JAPAN, INC., *Tokyo*
SIMON & SCHUSTER ASIA PTE. LTD., *Singapore*
EDITORA PRENTICE-HALL DO BRASIL, LTDA., *Rio de Janeiro*

Contents

2   *Middle Elementary Grades*   30

3 Upper Elementary Grades 66

Appendix   123

Index of Songs   127

Index of Poems   129

Preface

Orff-Schulwerk can be defined as a pedagogy to organize elements of music for children through speaking, singing, playing, and dancing. Carl Orff described his approach as an "idea" and as a "wild flower," conveying the thought that through nurturing, a wildflower will flourish yet maintain its identity.

Orff-Schulwerk began in 1924, when Carl Orff (1895–1982), a German composer, and Dorothee Günther, a specialist in dance, opened the Günther-schule in Munich to explore gymnastics, rhythmic dance, and expressive dance in combination with music. The result was a center where musicians and dancers worked together creatively. Musicians learned to express musical ideas in movement; dancers learned to sing and play. The totality of moving, singing, and playing instruments was an everpresent reality in a highly creative environment. This integrated group of dancers and musicians toured throughout Europe and were active until 1945, when the Güntherschule was bombed.

The foundation that the Güntherschule established was the integration of music with movement, with creativity always in the forefront. During the early stages, Gunild Keetman was integral to the Schulwerk development. Orff described her as a person with natural talent in equal parts for movement and music. He said of Keetman, "I am not exaggerating when I say that without Keetman's decisive contribution through her double talent, 'Schulwerk' could not have come into being."

Although the Güntherschule was no longer active after the war, the concepts it had developed were still alive. In 1948, Bavarian Radio asked Orff and his colleagues to present a series of broadcasts using the ideas of Schulwerk with children. Gunild Keetman was largely responsible for preparing the broadcasts, which were extremely successful. Teachers throughout Germany requested tapes and wanted to know how they could recreate these activities with children. The broadcasts eventually led to the publication of five volumes entitled *Orff-Schulwerk: Musik für Kinder* (Schott, Mainz, 1950–1954). These "original" volumes are sequential, beginning with melodies of two notes and rhythms in duple meter using quarter-note and eighth-note values. They progress melodically, rhythmically, and harmonically to encompass what is termed elemental music. Orff intended that these volumes be the "models" for leading children toward musical development. Surely, he was pleased to know before his death in 1982 that his ideas, used throughout the world, had been translated into every major language and adapted to a multitude of cultures.

Within the word *model* lies not only an example but also the possibility of development, extension, and creativity. The word itself implies a pattern; a clearer definition might be "a pattern to be adapted."

This adaptability is a beauty of teaching within the concepts of Orff-Schulwerk, but it is also a problem. Some teachers interpret the Orff approach as a system that lacks structure. A precise structure, if defined by step-by-step procedures, could be destructive to the nurturing of creative elements. Yet those teachers who think there is no structure are also badly misinformed. It is the balance between structure and freedom that must, at all times, be respected.

The elements of music used in Orff-Schulwerk are rhythm, melody, harmony, and timbre. Combining the elements into small forms—A, AB, ABA, rondo—makes the material work in musical ways.

Orff pedagogy appeals to the teacher who does not mind accepting the challenge of trying new ways to reach musical goals. Many teachers, though attracted to the ideas because they see the value of integrating singing, playing, dancing, and creating, feel insecure in some areas, particularly in movement and creativity. Those who take "one small step at a time" will find many initial fears ill-founded. It is the secure teacher who knows that even the best-planned lessons are not always perfect. It is the teacher who is willing to take risks and then evaluate lessons carefully who will grow and find Schulwerk a mode for musical growth.

WHAT THIS BOOK DOES NOT DO

One cannot completely understand Orff-Schulwerk teaching by reading or teaching from materials in this book. Although the materials are sequenced and presented from a standpoint of child development, some classes will need more than a single experience before moving to more complex ideas. Training for Orff teachers is essential, and it is available throughout the United States in summer courses offered as Introductory, Level I, Level II, and Level III. A teacher who participates in three levels of training over three years will experience all the possibilities inherent in teaching in the "elemental style."

This book does not assume the task of training children to be individually skilled performers. Orff-Schulwerk is an approach to group teaching. It allows opportunity for every child to be involved from the moment class begins. With the teacher as a guide, children with high skill levels and children less skilled can participate simultaneously. The hope of an Orff teacher is that through carefully planned lessons, children will attain well-rounded musical experiences. These experiences can be an excellent foundation for individual study, but individual study is not a goal. Certainly, it has been shown that integrated musical experiences, such as those Orff offers, provide strong rhythmic and ear-training skills for band, orchestra, and choral ensembles at the high school level.

This book does not include "art" music, such as compositions by Beethoven and Bach. Integrated experiences in listening, done in "active" ways, should be explored, but that in itself is another book. Likewise, teaching the skill of playing the recorder is not a focus of this book. That is not to say that establishing class instruction on the recorder is not advisable. The author highly encourages this, particularly for upper elementary students.

It is important to say that this book is not a day-by-day curriculum. Although a curriculum used as a guide is laudable, a curriculum can become a dictator. A curriculum that must be followed can provide excuses for teachers who forget to evaluate daily progress; it can provide a reason for not allowing time for individual development; it can provide an alibi for glossing over unaccomplished skills. There is an enormous danger in having a tightly developed curriculum that allows for minimal flexibility because individual classes at the same grade level are seldom at the same place developmentally, and a class rarely accomplishes exactly what the previous class accomplished the year before.

Last, there is another volume waiting to be written for the junior high student.

Konnie K. Saliba

Definition of Terms

Body percussion   Body sounds used to create or reproduce rhythmic patterns. Levels of body percussion most frequently used include snapping fingers, clapping hands, patting knees, and stamping feet.

Bordun (simple)   An accompaniment based upon tonic and dominant, sounding as a pedal point below the melody.

Convergent rhythms   Rhythms that occur on the pulse.

Divergent rhythms   Rhythms that do not occur on the pulse, such as dotted notes and syncopations.

Inner hearing; Internalization   To hear melody, words, or both in the mind, without external sound.

Ostinato   A repeated rhythmic, melodic, or harmonic pattern.
   Ostinati: More than one ostinato.
   Layered ostinati: Ostinati added one-by-one.

Pentatonic scale   A five-tone scale. In Orff-Schulwerk, the most frequently used pentatonic scales are five tones without half steps. The major pentatonics—C, F, and G—are DRM SL. The minor pentatonics—A, D, and G—are L DRM S.

Sound carpet   Use of Orff instruments as a background for speech, song, or movement. Possibilities include glissandos, tremolos, and random unpitched percussion sounds.

Introduction

What then, is elemental music? Never music alone, but music connected with movement, dance, and speech—not to be listened to, meaningful only in active participation. Elemental music is pre-intellectual, it lacks great form, its contents earthy, natural, almost a physical activity. It can be learned and enjoyed by anyone. It is fitting for children. (Carl Orff)

This book provides materials and suggestions for teaching music to children in grades 1–6. The categories of rhythm, melody, movement, and playing instruments are divided into lower, middle, and upper elementary sections, thereby sequencing the material. But despite the organization of this book, or of any book, it is important that the teacher have thorough knowledge of the nature of children and of their capabilities. For example, the teacher should know that the young child is comfortable singing in a limited range, should have multiple experiences in pulse-related activities, should experience rhythms without complications, needs to use the hands simultaneously before alternating them when playing an instrument, is intrigued by the mystery of a story, and is fascinated by the "magic" sound of the Orff instruments. If the training for the young child is thorough, the foundation is secure. Then, gradually, each facet of music training can be increased in scope and difficulty. It is very possible for fifth- and sixth-grade students to provide song accompaniments consisting of multiple-ostinato patterns and to create the dance and designate the form. Such highly developed activities are not practical for first- and second-grade students.

When planning lessons using the Orff approach, it is important to remember that experience precedes conceptualization. In traditional approaches to teaching music, rhythmic and melodic notation are beginning points; through a deductive method, the child comes to know about music. Orff-Schulwerk is an inductive approach in which multiple experiences in speech, rhythm, moving, singing, and playing are integrated so that children make and participate in music before learning how music is notated.

It is important to realize that children are not observers in an Orff class; they are the active participants. From the moment class begins, the children should be involved. When using the Orff approach, the teacher must be cognizant that this is not individual teaching but group teaching, and that all children are taught all parts.

Rhythm is the primary component of musical expression, but rhythm does not stand alone; it is body-related and connected with speech, with movement, with song. For children, it is natural to use the body as a means of expressing rhythm.

Singing should be a primary focus for all Orff teachers. Having an array of percussion instruments should not serve as an excuse for not training the singing voice. The teacher is free to use solfeggio, a neutral syllable, numbers, or letter names. In kindergarten and first grade, tone-matching games should occur in each lesson. Children in first and second grades should be able to hear a melodic pattern and echo-sing it correctly. They should be continuously presented with appropriate folk melodies to expand their repertoire. By the upper grades, children should be singing ostinato patterns with a melody and eventually should sing in harmony. Throughout the training of the singing voice, the teacher should focus on correct posture, breathing, enunciation, and a clear tone, free of tension. The creative Orff teacher uses many ways to train the singing voice but never neglects this aspect of music education.

Children love to express themselves in movement. The creative teacher can find a multitude of ways to include this vital element, such as movement to accompany singing, gestures with the body, creative movement with or without sound, and, of course, dance. Movement should be encouraged and nurtured, from exploration for the young child to form and structure for the upper elementary student.

The Orff instrumentarium was inspired by instruments from Africa (xylophones, wood instruments, drums); Europe (recorders, glockenspiels, Renaissance instruments); Asia (metallophones, metal percussion); and the Americas (jazz percussion, bass, Latin percussion). The models designed for children are smaller and have removable bars, enabling them to be arranged in a variety of pentatonic, major, and minor scales. Although the instruments can be used to educate, they are also poetic in sound. They can be used by the youngest child to provide a soft background or a childlike accompaniment, and by the more advanced student as a rich accompaniment. They are "magic" in sound, and this does not escape the imagination of the child.

It is the responsibility of the music teacher to help children learn the language of music. Because children learn in different ways, the teacher should provide multiple and continuing experiences to further musical growth. This training includes rhythm, melody, harmony, and movement. It has structure, freedom, theory, and creativity. The author hopes that the teaching will include joy, resulting in experiences for children to last a lifetime.

He who knows nothing, loves nothing. He who can do nothing understands nothing. He who understands nothing is worthless. But he who understands also loves, notices, sees. . . . The more knowledge is inherent in a thing, the greater the love. . . . Anyone who imagines that all fruits ripen at the same time as the strawberries knows nothing about grapes. (Paracelsus)

1

Lower Elementary Grades

Rhythm

For the child below the age of seven years, the most important note values to be experienced are the quarter note, the eighth note, and the half note. Be aware that young children need to experience rhythm at their body tempo; since the young child has a fast heartbeat, that tempo will be considerably faster than an adult tempo. The young child is comfortable working in meters of 2/♩ and 6/♪, as can be verified by the wealth of nursery rhymes and playground chants in those meters. The creative teacher will "make haste slowly" with children below the age of seven to be certain the fundamentals of rhythm are secure before moving to more advanced concepts. While working with children using quarter, eighth, and half notes, you should also encourage kinesthetic response to finding the underlying pulse, a prerequisite to ensemble playing that will occur at the middle and upper elementary levels. The teacher of lower elementary ages should select material that is (1) rhythmically convergent (words occurring on the pulse); (2) short enough to be learned aurally (four-line poems or two-phrase songs are ideal); and (3) psychologically appropriate for the young child.

RHYTHM IN MOVEMENT [♩ (♩ ♪), ♩, and ♫]

ACTIVITIES

Duck (♩)

Chickies (♫)

Goose (♩)

1. Point to a picture and speak rhythmically; have children speak with you.

2. Have the children add a kinesthetic activity by patting their knees while speaking.

3. Create a speech phrase (8 counts) such as "goose, goose, goose, goose"; afterwards, have the children move in space with the rhythm in their feet.

4. Improvise at the piano using the low register for ♩, the middle register for ♪, and the high register for ♫. Silence at the keyboard is an indication for the children to "freeze."

5. Divide the class into three parts. One-third move only when hearing ♩; one-third on ♪; and one-third on ♫. Switch groups.

6. Improvise at the piano or move in space combining ♩♩ or ♩♫ or ♩♩♩ into an 8-beat phrase. Have the children listen, or watch, and then verbally describe what you have done.
   For example: ♩♩♩♩♩♩ = duck, duck, duck, duck, goose, goose.

7. Use three distinctly different timbres, one for each note value, and ask the children to respond in movement. For example: ♩ = cymbal, ♪ = temple blocks, ♫ = sleigh bells.

RHYTHM IN SPEECH (♩ and ♪)

ACTIVITIES

Proverbs

Keep calm, keep calm. Watch your step, yes, watch your step, yes

1. Have the children speak the two proverbs one after the other, using high voices for one and low voices for the other.

2. Have the children speak the proverbs while adding locomotor movement.

3. Have the children speak the proverbs first and then internalize[1] them while moving in space.

WAYS TO WORK WITH PULSE (♩, ♫, and ♩)

ACTIVITIES

---

1. The "Hi" Game

Begin with a pulse somewhere on the body (for example, the knees) and have the children join. Then move the location of the pulse (for example, to the shoulders). The children may not change their pulse location until they hear the word "Hi."

Variation: Use ♩, ♫, or ♩ on different parts of the body.

2. Using Names as Building Blocks

Group four first names together. Choose names that reinforce the note values of ♩, ♫, and ♩. For example:

Gre-gor-y,   An-tho-ny,   Car-o-lyn,   Sue.

[1]See Definition of Terms, in the front matter of this text.

Have the children add a pulse (♩) patted on the knees. Let them speak once in high voices and once in low voices. Consider adding a second group of names, such as:

Sam-my, Ma-ry, Jim-my, An-gie.

Have the children add a pulse patted on knees and whisper this set of names. Combine the two sets into an ABA form.

3. Using an Object

Poem

One, two, let's play a game.
When you catch the ball, tell us your name.

Have the class stand in a circle, with you in the center. All speak the words rhythmically while you toss the ball on the pulse to different children.

4. Using a Poem

Poem

To market, to market to buy a fat <u>pig</u>.

Home again, home again, dancing a <u>jig</u>.

To market, to market to buy a fat hog,

Home again, home again, jiggety jog.

Speak the poem and have the class add a pulse by patting knees with both hands at once or by alternating hands. Divide the class into two groups. All speak while one group provides the pulse on knees and the other group claps on the rhyming words <u>pig</u> and <u>jig</u> and stamps on hog and jog.

To extend the activity:

a.   Transfer claps and stamps to two different unpitched percussion instruments.
b.   Choose a child to skip in the space for the length of the poem, returning to his or her place in the class by the last word.

5. Using a Poem and Adding Inner Hearing[2]

Poem

It's <u>raining</u>, it's <u>pouring</u>,
The old man is <u>snoring</u>.
He went to bed and bumped his <u>head</u>
And couldn't get up in the <u>morning</u>.

Write the words of the poem on a visual. Have the children speak in unison, using a variety of vocal inflection. Add a pulse by patting knees and clapping hands:

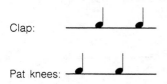

[2]See Definition of Terms.

Ask the class to speak only the underlined words while thinking the other words and maintaining the pulse accompaniment.

To extend the activity:

 a. Transfer the pulse accompaniment to two timpani.

 b. Transfer the underlined words to an unpitched percussion instrument, such as a triangle.

6. Using a Poem with ♩, ♪, and ♫ as Accompaniment

Poem

1. There was a man lived in the moon,
 Lived in the moon, lived in the moon.
 There was a man lived in the moon,
 His name was Aiken Drum.

2. His hat was made of good green cheese,
 Good green cheese, good green cheese.
 His hat was made of good green cheese,
 His name was Aiken Drum.

3. His coat was made of good roast beef,
 Good roast beef, good roast beef.
 His coat was made of good roast beef,
 His name was Aiken Drum.

4. His buttons were made of penny loaves,
 Penny loaves, penny loaves.
 His buttons were made of penny loaves,
 His name was Aiken Drum.

Have the children pat their knees, using a half-note pulse for verse 1, a quarter-note pulse for verse 2, an eighth-note pulse for verse 3.

Suggestion for verse four: Divide the class into three groups. Assign the half-note pulse to one group, the quarter-note pulse to the second, and the eighth-note pulse to the third. Have the groups perform simultaneously.

7. Using a Song with ♩, ♪, and ♫ as Accompaniments on Unpitched Percussion Instruments

SONG OF THE CLOCKS

Konnie Saliba

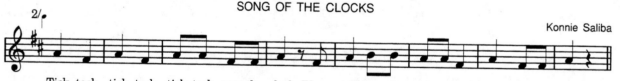

Tick, tock, tick, tock, tick, tock, says the clock. Please tell me what time it is, Grand-fa-ther clock.

Have the children add the pulse pattern ♩ (ding, dong), first as knee pats, then transferred to a cymbal.

Have the children clap the pulse pattern ♩ (tick, tock) and then transfer it to a wood block.

Have the children snap the pulse pattern ♫ (tick-a, tock-a) and then transfer it to claves.

EXPERIENCES WITH CONVERGENT RHYTHMIC STRUCTURES (METERS 2/♩ AND 6/♪)

ACTIVITIES

---

1. Developing Word Chains from Familiar Topics

Ro-bin, Blue-jay, Wood-peck-er, Owl,

Pur-ple mar-tin, Chick-a - dee, Hum-ming-bird, Wren.

If possible, use a picture for each bird. The order shown is one possibility. Allow the children to rearrange the order. Have them clap the rhythm of the sequence and then transfer it to temple blocks. Have them add a pulse accompaniment (♩♪) as knee pats; transfer to timpani. Develop a form. For example: A = speech only; A_1 = rhythm clapped; A_2 = rhythm on temple blocks; all accompanied by timpani.

2. Using Body Percussion as a Pulse Game for a Poem in 2/

Poem

Pease por-ridge hot.   Pease por-ridge cold.

Pease por-ridge in the pot, Nine days old.

Some like it   hot,   Some like it   cold,

Some like it   in the pot, Nine days old.

Body Percussion

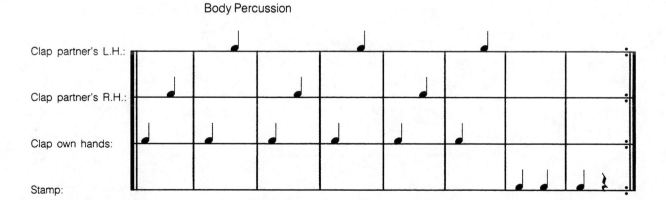

Clap partner's L.H.:

Clap partner's R.H.:

Clap own hands:

Stamp:

Divide the class into partners. Allow students to practice the body percussion part without speaking; then have them add the words.

To extend the activity: Have the children internalize the words and move silently to new partners for a repeat of the game.

3. Using Body Percussion as a Pulse Game for a Poem in 6/8

Poem

Lit-tle Miss Muf - fet   Sat on a   tuf - fet,

Eat-ing her curds and   whey.   A - long came a spi-der and

sat down be-side her, And fright-ened Miss Muf-fet a - way.

Body Percussion

Snap:

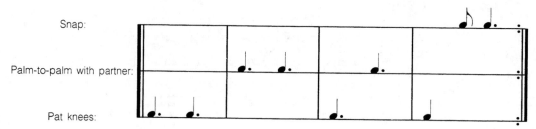

Palm-to-palm with partner:

Pat knees:

Divide the class into partners. Allow the students to practice the body percussion part without speaking. Have them add the words.

To extend the activity: As an interlude, play two phrases of the 6/8 pulse on a hand drum while the children skip in space to find new partners.

4. Recognizing Lines That Are Alike

Poem

2/4 Deedle deedle dumpling, my son John.

Went to bed with his <u>stockings on</u>.

One shoe (off,)

One shoe (on,)

Deedle deedle dumpling, my son John.

Have the children clap the rhythm of the first and last lines, using finger snapping for "stockings on" and a stamp for the words "off" and "on." Have them transfer the three levels of body percussion to three unpitched percussion instruments. Develop a form. For example: A = speech; A_1 = speech and unpitched instruments; A_2 = unpitched percussion instruments only.

5. Using a Poem for Ensemble Experience

Poem

2/♩ or 6/♪   One, Two, Buckle my shoe.
Three, Four, Shut the door.
Five, Six, Pick up sticks.
Seven, Eight, Lay them straight.
Nine, Ten, A big fat hen.

Suggestions for development:

a. Divide the class into two sections. Section 1 speaks numbers; section 2 completes each sentence.
b. Have the class clap numbers and pat other words on knees.
c. Transfer words to unpitched percussion instruments.
d. Have all the children step each number and pantomime other words.

6. Adding an Introduction and a Coda to a Poem

Poem

6/♪

Doc-tor Fos-ter went to Glouces-ter

In   a show-er of   rain.

He stepped in a pud-dle,   up to his mid-dle,

And nev-er went there a - gain.

Have the children speak the poem rhythmically with good vocal inflection. Add a pulse accompaniment on body percussion or timpani. Add an introduction.

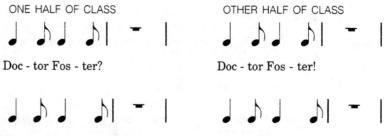

ONE HALF OF CLASS   OTHER HALF OF CLASS

Doc - tor Fos - ter?   Doc - tor Fos - ter!

Went to Glouces-ter?   Went to Glouces-ter!

Add a coda (unison speech).

A - gain,   a - gain,   He   nev-er went there a - gain!

Melody

DEVELOPING THE VOICE

The first instrument to be developed is the voice. Begin with a simple motif in a comfortable vocal range. A good key for the preschool-aged child is D major. However, for light, in-tune singing, the goal should be the key of F major.

With young children, the first melodic concept to work with is that of high and low. Ways to approach this include

1. Speech, in high and low voices
2. Movement, corresponding to the high and the low registers of the piano, moving on tiptoes and with knees bent
3. Relating the sound of a triangle to finger snapping, the sound of the bass drum to stamps

With the young child, begin with two- and three-note melodies. The two-note, bitonic melody is intimate and psychologically attuned to the age of the child. It is an interval that goes from high to low; it is the interval of the "childhood chant" found throughout the world. It is suggested that solfeggio be used.

Provide opportunities for young children to match tones with you. One way to do that is to sing in the child's range with a light tone (begin in the key of D major). Avoid using the piano to accompany singing.

TONE MATCHING

ACTIVITIES

1. Using a Puppet

Introduce a hand puppet to the class. Be sure to give the puppet a name. The puppet ("Sammy," for example) sings hello to the entire class, using the falling third (A to F-sharp). Sammy can also sing to individual children such things as the day of the week, a description of the weather, and what holiday is coming soon.

2. Question-Answer Game

All the children are seated in a circle with their hands open behind their backs. The teacher has a penny, a pencil, and a key, and places one each in the open hands of three children. The singing game then is:

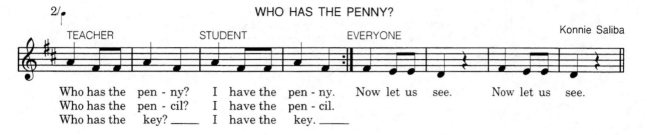

WHO HAS THE PENNY?

Konnie Saliba

TEACHER · STUDENT · EVERYONE

Who has the pen - ny? I have the pen - ny. Now let us see. Now let us see.
Who has the pen - cil? I have the pen - cil.
Who has the key? ____ I have the key. ____

3. Grouping Names

Select four children and create a phrase using their first names.

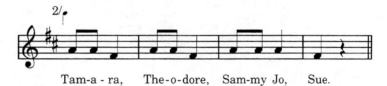

Tam-a - ra, The-o-dore, Sam-my Jo, Sue.

Each child may sing individually, with the class echo-singing, or everyone in the class may sing all the names in sequence.

BITONIC MELODY

ACTIVITIES

CLAP, SNAP, AND SHAKE

Konnie Saliba

Clap up high,   Clap down low,   Turn a-round,   Touch the ground.
Snap up high,   Snap down low,   Turn a-round,   Touch the ground.
Shake up high,   Shake down low,   Turn a-round,   Touch the ground.
Stand   tall,   Stand   low,   Turn a-round,   Now sit down.

Have the children add gestures and movement during the rests.

Have the children add a bordun[3] accompaniment on the pulse, using alto or bass xylophone.

BORDUN:
Bass Xylophone

SPRING AND FALL

Konnie Saliba

Spring is   here,   Spring is   here.   Birds and   flow - ers   now ap - pear.
Fall   is   here,   Fall   is   here.   Birds and   flow - ers   dis - ap - pear.

[3]See Definition of Terms.

Precede the song with creative movement. All the children can move as birds, or grow as flowers might in a spring garden. Ask the children to sing verse 1 and then internalize the words, using inner hearing, while performing the movement. For the movement verses, add to the experience by improvising for the length of the melody on a metallophone in the scale of F pentatonic (B's and E's removed from the instrument).

BIRDS

Blue-bird,   Black-bird,   Car-di-nal,   Crow.
Ro - bin,   Spar-row,   O - ri - ole,   Owl.

Each measure with an asterisk (*) can be rhythmically duplicated on one or more unpitched percussion instruments. The song can also be extended by preceding it with the "Spring and Fall" song.

RAIN, RAIN, GO AWAY

Traditional

Rain,   rain,   go   a - way,   Come   a - gain   a - no - ther   day.
Did   you   see my (frog?) Sit - ting   there   up - on   a   (log?)
I   just   saw him dash.   Next   I   heard   a   great   big   splash!

After the children have learned the song by rote, have them sing verse 1 and internalize it. Have them do the same for verse 2, clapping on the words "frog" and "log." Add finger snaps for "dash" and "splash." Transfer this preparation to instruments as follows:

After verse 1: Glockenspiels improvise in F pentatonic (B's and E's removed).

After verse 2: Play rhyming words on guiro.

After verse 3: Play an upward glissando on xylophones for the words "dash" and "splash."

TRITONIC MELODY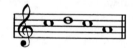

ACTIVITIES

_____

BELL HORSES

Traditional

Bell hor-ses, Bell hor-ses, What's the time of day?   One o'clock, two o'clock, time to a - way.
Good hor-ses, bad hor-ses, What's the time of day?   Three o' clock, four o'clock time to a - way.

BORDUN:
Bass Xylophone

Add sleigh bells playing eighth notes, and an alto or a bass xylophone playing a bordun accompaniment on the pulse. Add an introduction on a triangle, striking the time the song is to begin (two o'clock, four o'clock, and so on).

BYE BABY BUNTING

Traditional

Bye ba - by bun - ting. Dad - dy's gone a - hunt - ing. To catch a lit - tle rab - bit skin, To wrap the ba - by bunt - ing in.

BORDUN:
Bass Xylophone

Prepare the words "bunting" and "hunting" by having the children clap each syllable; transfer the claps to a triangle. Prepare the words "rabbit skin" and "bunting in" by having the children pat their knees; transfer pats to a wood block. Let the class sing the song with unpitched instruments. Ask them to internalize the words and use only unpitched instruments in the correct places.

GHOST SONG

Konnie Saliba

Green ghost, green ghost, Who do you see? I see a blue ghost look-ing at me.
Blue ghost, blue ghost, Who do you see? I see a yellow ghost look-ing at me.

For this song, use a flannel board and pieces of flannel of different colors cut into the shape of ghosts. Before you sing the first phrase, place a green ghost on the flannel board. Before the answer phrase, which may be sung by the class, place a blue ghost next to the green one. This singing game can continue as long as you have colored ghosts. After all ghosts are on the flannel board, the answer for the last question can be whispered: "No One."

Variations: Use different animals or birds. Answers may be sung by individual children.

GIDDYUP, MY BURRO

New Mexico

Gid-dy-up, my bur-ro, we're go-ing to Be - lén. Fies-ta is to - mor-row and one next day a - gain.

Sleigh Bells:

BORDUN:
Bass Xylophone

Consider letting several children accompany with sleigh bells and alto or bass xylophone. You may add a B Section, using speech.

Come to the Fiesta,
Won't you come along?
Come to the Fiesta
And join us in our song.

Spanish Text:
Arre, mi burrito,
que vamos a Belén,
Que mañana es fiesta
y el otro también.

TETRATONIC MELODY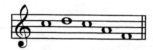

ACTIVITIES

READY FOR DINNER

Konnie Saliba

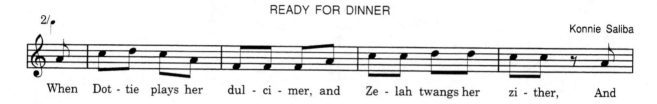

When Dot-tie plays her dul-ci-mer, and Ze-lah twangs her zi-ther,   And

Tom-my plays his glock-en-spiel, we're rea-dy for our din-ner.

Have the children create an A₁ Section by putting all the nouns on unpitched percussion instruments and performing them without singing. Possible instruments are

Dottie	= Wood block
dulcimer	= Glissando on xylophone
Zelah	= Hand drum
zither	= Guiro
Tommy	= Tambourine
glockenspiel	= Glissando on glockenspiel

"CROAK," SAID THE TOAD

Konnie Saliba

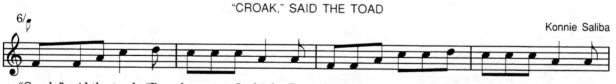

"Croak," said the toad, "I'm hun-gry, I think. To-day I've had no-thing to eat or to drink. I'll

crawl to the gar-den and jump through the pales, And there I'll dine nice-ly on slugs and on snails."

Divide the class into partners and add a pulse or a body percussion game to the singing.

Clap both of partner's hands:

Clap own hands:

Pat knees:

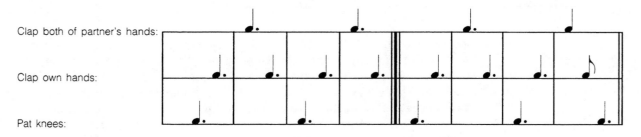

FOLKLORIC MELODY

ACTIVITIES

OLD MISTER RABBIT

Folk Song

Old   Mis - ter   Rab - bit,   you   got   a   migh - ty   ha - bit,   Of

jump - ing   in   my   gar - den   and ___   eat - ing   all   my   cab - bage.

Add rhythmic gestures to accompany the singing as follows:

Touch   shoulders.   Pat   knees.   Jump in place.   Clap hands.

HOP, OLD SQUIRREL

Folk Song

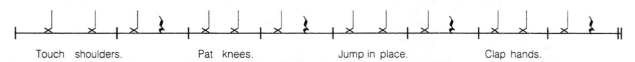

Hop, old squirrel,   ei-dle-dum, ei-dle-dum, Hop, old squirrel,   ei-dle-dum-dee!   ei-dle-dum-dee!

Add locomotor and nonlocomotor movement as follows:

Hop 3 times.   Move shoulders alternately.   Hop 3 times.   Move shoulders alternately.

Movement

Carl Orff once said, "Elemental music is never music alone but forms a unity with movement, dance, and speech." Movement is the key to rhythmic success. Children love to move, and the wise teacher guides these explorations to allow each child to develop in movement skills. It is important for the young child to experience the locomotor activities of walking, running, galloping, skipping, hopping, and jumping. Children should also be encouraged to explore nonlocomotor activities, such as bending, shaking, stretching, twisting, shrinking, and growing. Stopping-and-starting games are important, because children of this age need work in balancing skills. Teachers of children in the lower grades will want to work toward having everyone in the class stepping to a common beat. There should also be time for creative movement. Movement is a personal and an individual activity, because no one moves exactly as someone else does. A child feels good when he or she moves and will continually work to become more skilled. Movement should be a part of every music lesson.

LOCOMOTOR MOVEMENT

Stepping to a Beat

Ask a small group of children to walk in the space while you watch. Ask them to stop when they hear a drum signal. Try to find an average walking tempo among the small group and establish it as a walking pulse. For young children, this will be considerably faster than the tempo of an adult. If the space you are using is small, ask half the class to move to the drum beat while the other half pat their knees with the walking pulse. Then switch groups. Add a speech pattern:

Walk, Walk, Walk, Walk, Walk, and Stop!

Later, you will want to add variations to stepping to a beat. These can include

1. Levels: Movement can be at a standing level or on tiptoes or low to the ground.
2. Direction: Try moving backward, or include a pattern, such as a zigzag or a circle.
3. Dramatic ideas: Add an image. Instead of just walking to school, walk as if it is Friday and there is a class party! Or walk as if it is late at night and very dark outside. Add a feeling to the walk, such as sad, tired, happy. Become a character or an animal.

ACTIVITIES

Tell the children to walk low to the ground if they hear the low drum; walk high in the air with the high drum. Tell them to freeze into statues if they hear a rim tap.

Let the children walk anywhere in the room with the sound of the wood block. Each child should walk in his or her own circle with the sound of the hand drum.

Have the children walk low to the ground with the sounds being played in the low register of the piano. Have them walk on tiptoes with sounds in the high register.

Let the children walk in giant steps ($\quarternote$) and walking steps ($\quarternote$) and running steps ($\eighthnote\eighthnote$).

Have the children walk like elephants (♩) and bears (♩) and mice (♫).

Have the children vary the walk with short or long steps; with knees bent; with stiff knees, as a robot; with heavy accents; with light steps.

Teach the children a "Walking Song," which may incorporate some of the preceding activities.

WALKING SONG

Konnie Saliba

I can walk and walk and walk and walk and walk and then I stop!

Variations: Run, hop, jump.

Galloping

The gallop is a movement with the same foot forward. It is a movement that all preschool children and first-grade children enjoy doing.

ACTIVITIES

Play a 6/₈ rhythm on a hand drum. Ask the children to gallop as you play and to stop if the drum sound stops (♩. ♪ ♩. ♪).

Vary the galloping activity by also including patterns for walking (♩. ○).

Assign the timbre of a wood block to the gallop, that of a drum to the walk.

Divide the class into three groups and assign each to a corner of the room. Group 1 are elephants (○); they move only with the sound of the bass drum and go immediately back to their corner if the drum sound stops. Group 2 are kangaroos (♩.) and move with the sound of a suspended cymbal. Group 3 are ponies (♩. ♪) and move with the sound of the temple blocks. Change groups to allow each child to perform the three activities.

Speak the following poem and have the children gallop to it; or have the children both speak and gallop.

My horse can gallop,
My horse can gallop,
My horse can gallop and trot.
He trots up hills,
He trots down hills,
He trots and doesn't stop.
But when he gets hungry, you see,
He stops very suddenly.
He stops,
He stops,
He stops.

Skipping

By first grade, most, but not all, children can skip. Because skipping is a weight-change movement, it is more difficult than galloping. Plan activities for both skipping and galloping, but don't be surprised if some children gallop during a skipping activity.

ACTIVITIES

Practice walking, running, and skipping. Allow the children to suggest a sequence using those movements. For example: walk, walk, walk, skip, skip, skip; or, run, run, run, run, run run, run, run, skip, skip, stop.

Make an obstacle course in the room consisting of such things as a chair, a box, and an instrument. Allow each child to skip around each obstacle to reach a goal line. A drum beat may be added.

Create a game for speech and skipping. Have the children stand in a circle formation. The teacher stands inside the circle, holding a big paper lollipop. Select individual children to skip around the circle, trying to go around the circle and touch the lollipop while children in the circle are chanting:

Skip around the circle,
Skip and don't you stop.
Skip around the circle
And touch the lollipop.

Play a singing game, "Sally Go Round the Sun." All children are in a circle and a "Sally" is selected to skip around the outside of the circle while everyone sings. On the word "Boom," Sally selects a new person to skip around the circle, and Sally goes into the center of the circle and sits down. The game continues until all but one person are sitting in the center; the last person to skip then asks all to stand on the last word, "Boom."

SALLY GO ROUND THE SUN

Traditional

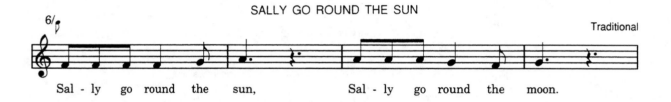

Sal - ly go round the sun,   Sal - ly go round the moon.

Sal - ly go round the chim - ney pot, on a Sun - day af - ter - noon. Boom!

Hopping

A hop is a movement on one foot. Children should be able to hop on one foot three times and then hop on the other without losing balance.

ACTIVITIES

Let the children help in assigning an unpitched percussion instrument for walking, skipping or galloping, and hopping. As you play one of the three instruments, children in the class move appropriately.

Create a speech sequence for hopping. (Stems up indicate to hop on one foot; stems down indicate to hop on the other foot. Let each child decide which foot to begin with.)

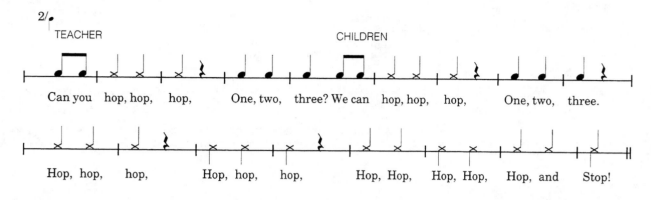

Can you hop, hop, hop, One, two, three? We can hop, hop, hop, One, two, three.

Hop, hop, hop, Hop, hop, hop, Hop, Hop, Hop, Hop, Hop, and Stop!

Add hopping and gestures to a song.

BUNNY FOO FOO

Traditional

Lit - tle Bun - ny Foo Foo, hop - ping through the for - est,
Lit - tle Bun - ny Foo Foo, I don't want to see you

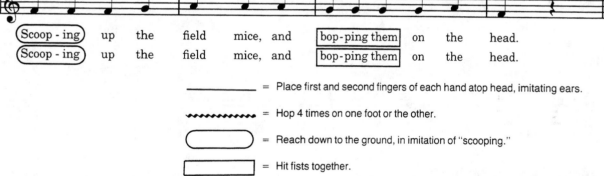

(Scoop - ing) up the field mice, and [bop-ping them] on the head.
(Scoop - ing) up the field mice, and [bop-ping them] on the head.

_____ = Place first and second fingers of each hand atop head, imitating ears.

〜〜〜〜〜 = Hop 4 times on one foot or the other.

( ) = Reach down to the ground, in imitation of "scooping."

[ ] = Hit fists together.

Jumping

A jump is a movement that uses both feet. Children frequently like to use the movement to see who among them can jump the farthest.

ACTIVITIES

Ask each child to imagine that he or she is standing in the center of a mud puddle. Suggest activities based upon the space the mud puddle occupies. For example:

  a. Jump out of the mud puddle; walk around it once and jump back into the mud puddle.
  b. Jump out of the mud puddle; walk low to the ground around the puddle and hop back into the mud puddle.
  c. Stretch very tall in the mud puddle and then jump three times in the puddle, scattering the mud.

Speak the following poem.

3/♩   Jack be nimble
      Jack be quick.
      Jack jump over
      The candlestick.

As everyone speaks, let each child in the class walk, skip, or gallop to a candle holder placed on the floor, and then jump over it, either during the word "over" or by the end of the rhyme.

Make a speech-and-movement game for the following sequence. For variation, eliminate the words and substitute a different unpitched percussion instrument for each locomotor movement.

I can jump,   jump,   jump, jump, jump. I can hop,   hop,   hop, hop, hop.

I can run and run and run and run and run and run and run. I can walk,   walk, and then I   stop.

For example:

JUMP IN, JUMP OUT

Konnie Saliba

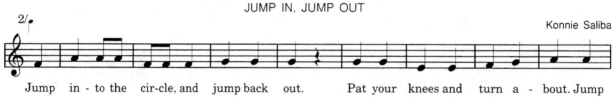

Jump   in - to the   cir-cle, and   jump back   out.   Pat your   knees and   turn a - bout. Jump

in,   jump   out, jump   in,   jump   out.   Pat your   knees and   turn a - bout.

NONLOCOMOTOR MOVEMENT

Plan many short activities to allow the children to experiment with and enjoy nonlocomotor movement. It is a good way to provide opportunities for children to relax, which helps to eliminate tension. Taking a minute to allow children to shake their hands vigorously in the air—up high, down low, in front of and behind the body—will help the entire class to relax enough to focus on learning activities. It is also important that children know how their bodies are joined at the neck, elbow, wrist, waist, knee, and ankle.

ACTIVITIES

Play a "Puppet" game to help children know which parts of their bodies will bend. Ask each child to imagine that he or she is a puppet and that all parts of the body that bend are controlled by strings that you hold. At first, name each body part that is lifted or released by a string. Later, give a drum signal and have the children release or add imaginary strings to parts of the body they select.

Add a poem to a bending activity. Ask the children to select one or more parts of the body that will bend while they are speaking:

2/ I've hinges that bend
From my toes to my head.
If my hinges didn't bend,
I'd most likely be dead!

Sing the following song, and ask the children to suggest what they might do when they all go out to play. Some model suggestions include:

a. We'll wave our arms.
b. We'll bend our knees.
c. We'll all play ball.
d. We'll shrink and grow.

WHAT SHALL WE DO?

American Traditional

What shall we do when we all go out? All go out? All go out?

When we all go out to play?

For the following song, choose a child to be the leader. During measures 1 and 2, the leader adds gesture or nonlocomotor movement. All join the leader. During the last two measures, the leader touches or points to a successor, who begins the game again.

THIS IS WHAT I CAN DO

Traditional

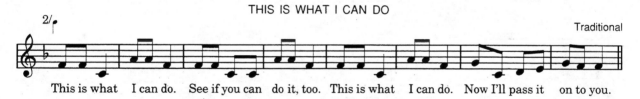

This is what I can do. See if you can do it, too. This is what I can do. Now I'll pass it on to you.

Have the children sing and perform the following song.

GONNA SHAKE OUT MY HANDS

American Folk Song

Gon - na shake out my hands, gon - na shake out my hands.

Gon - na shake 'em high, shake 'em low, shake out my hands.

Variations: Shake out arms, feet, legs.

Have the children sing and perform the following song.

WATCH AND SEE

Konnie Saliba

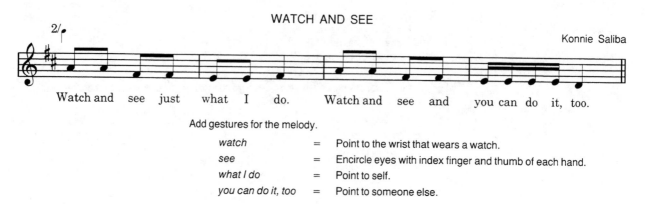

Watch and see just what I do. Watch and see and you can do it, too.

Add gestures for the melody.

watch	=	Point to the wrist that wears a watch.
see	=	Encircle eyes with index finger and thumb of each hand.
what I do	=	Point to self.
you can do it, too	=	Point to someone else.

Add a B Section.

B SECTION

TEACHER: Shake, shake, shake, shake, shake both your hands.
CLASS: Shake, shake, shake, shake, shake, both our hands.

Variations: Add nonlocomotor movements, such as twist, bend, shrink, grow, punch, slash, and rock.

TRADITIONAL GAMES

ONE FINGER, ONE THUMB

American Folk Song

One fin - ger, one thumb keep mov - ing. One fin - ger, one thumb keep mov - ing.

One fin - ger, one thumb keep mov - ing, We'll all be hap - py and bright.

Verses: One finger, one thumb, one foot
One finger, one thumb, one foot, one elbow
One finger, one thumb, one foot, one elbow, one head
Etc.

MY HANDS KEEP MOVING

American Folk Song
(adapted)

All day my hands keep mov - ing, keep mov - ing, keep mov - ing. All day my hands keep

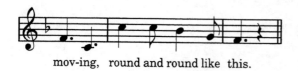

mov-ing, round and round like this.

Verses: arms keep moving . . . back and forth
    knees keep bending . . . up and down
    fingers keep tapping . . . on my knees
    heart keeps beating . . . on and on
    All of me keeps turning . . . round and round

PRETTY TRAPPINGS

American Folk Song

I can move one foot, but the o-ther's good for no-thing. I can move one foot,

but the o-ther is no good.

Verses: I can move one leg, arm, hand, knee, eye, *etc.*

Using Orff Instruments

Instrumental experiences for young children should include

1. Hearing how an instrument sounds
2. Learning how instruments should be played
3. Linking instrumental use, with songs and poems, to the pulse or the text

Take time to demonstrate how to play each unpitched percussion instrument. Show the children how to hold a hand drum in one hand and strike it near the rim to produce the best sound, rather than playing in the center, where the sound is dull. When playing instruments with mallets, such as temple blocks, piccolo blocks, slit drums, or barred instruments, children should be encouraged to play with alternate hands and loose wrists, grasping the mallets with the thumb and forefinger and turning the elbows outward slightly. Instruments such as a triangle or finger cymbals require more finely developed motor skills: One hand assumes the striking role while the other is stationary. When playing such an instrument, a child who is not certain of his or her dominant hand should play the instrument with a partner. One child holds the instrument while the other plays.

EXPLORATION OF UNPITCHED PERCUSSION AND BARRED INSTRUMENTS

ACTIVITIES

2/♪   Drums, drums, listen to the drums,
    Big drums, little drums, listen to the drums.

    Woods, woods, listen to the woods,
    Big woods, little woods, listen to the woods.

    Bells, bells, listen to the bells.
    Big bells, little bells, listen to the bells.

Have the children learn the preceding three verses by rote. Have them speak the drum verse in a low voice, the woods in a middle-range voice, the bells in a high voice. Let them speak each verse adding a pulse on the knees for drums, on the shoulders for woods, and on the head for bells. Then have them speak each verse with the pulse; internalize words for each verse using pulse on the body only. This is the preparation for using the instruments.

Divide the instruments into three groups—drums, woods, and metals. Have the children speak verse 1 with the pulse on the drums; internalize verse 1, using pulse only; and so on. Allow the children to change instruments for a repeat of the three verses.

A Word Chain for Metal Instruments

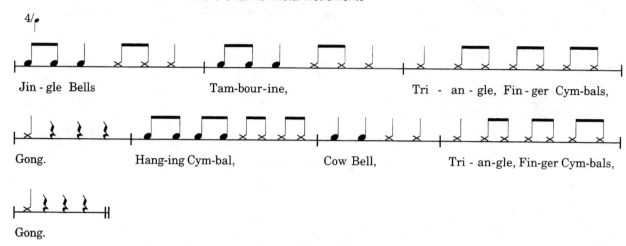

Jin - gle Bells   Tam-bour-ine,   Tri - an-gle, Fin-ger Cym-bals,

Gong.   Hang-ing Cym-bal,   Cow Bell,   Tri - an-gle, Fin-ger Cym-bals,

Gong.

Have the children use speech only with the regular notation; have them play the appropriate instrument with the ♩ notation. Suggestions include performing the word chain with speech and then internalizing the words, allowing the children to hear only instrumental timbre.

A Story for Wood Instruments

Late one evening, after a very long day, I was very tired. I dreamed I went to a store that was filled with *the most interesting things!* There were wonderful sounds all around me. There were clocks in all sizes and shapes. There was

the grandfather clock   (wood block ♩ 𝄽)
a grandmother clock   (two-tone wood block ♩ ♩)
tiny cuckoo clocks   (claves ♫ ♫)

There was a frog, but he looked like a fish! (guiro), and a cat sharpening her claws (sand blocks). There was a beautiful wooden pony (temple blocks) and my favorite of all, a toy train (maracas, cabaza, shakers). Every once in a while, the train would whistle (train whistle). There was a large goose, who wandered about looking at things (vibraslap). And yes, a tiny mouse who scurried about (piccolo blocks) with a mechanical robot, who occasionally tried to swat at him (whip). *What fun!!!* "Before I wake up," said I, "do you think you could play all those wonderful sounds all at the same time?"

Use half-note, quarter-note, and eighth-note rhythms for the clocks. The children can play the other instruments in an improvisatory manner as the story is read. At the end, begin with the clocks and add the other wood sounds, one at a time.

Rhythmic Speech for Drums

2/♩   Trum, trum, trum. See me play the hand drum.
Trum, trum, trum. See me play the drum.
Drums are fun, fun are the drums,
Trum, trum, trum. See me play the drum.

Young children may speak the poem and play only on the word "trum." The speech can also be combined with walking to the pulse. If other kinds of drums are used, all could be played on the word "trum," and only hand drums on other words.

Song, with Improvisation on Barred Instruments

WEATHER SONG

Konnie Saliba

Wind, play me a song.
Rain, play me a song.

Clouds, play me a song.
Ev - 'ry-one, play me a song.

Put the xylophones, metallophones, and glockenspiels in C pentatonic (remove all F's and B's). After singing the phrase about the wind, allow children playing xylophones to improvise; after singing the phrase about clouds, those playing metallophones improvise; after rain, those playing glockenspiels improvise.

CREATING A SOUND CARPET AS AN INTRODUCTION AND A CODA

ACTIVITIES

THE WOODPECKER

Folk Song (adapted)

Tap-a tap-a tap, Tap-a tap-a tap, Who can that be?

Tap-a tap-a tap, Tap-a tap-a tap, It's a wood-peck-er in the tree.

For the song itself, give the children wood unpitched percussion instruments and have them play the words "tap-a tap-a tap" while singing and later without singing. Put all the barred instruments into F pentatonic (remove B's and E's). Create a story for the woodpecker: He lives in the forest, and it is early in the morning when all his friends are just awakening, and so on. Children playing barred instruments may select any two notes and tremolo softly. Other sounds you may add to the "carpet" include the woodpecker (occasional tapping sounds on one temple block), a cricket (the cabaza), a frog (vibraslap), and the wind (rubbing the skin of a hand drum).

LINKING INSTRUMENTS TO WORDS

Using Barred Instruments and Unpitched Percussion Instruments

ACTIVITIES

Jack and Jill went up the hill

To fetch a pail of /water./

Jack fell down and broke his crown

And Jill came tumbling after.

Then up Jack got and off did trot

As fast as he could caper

To old Dame Dob who patched his nob

With vinegar and brown paper.
× × ×

For the youngest children, teach only the first four lines, and teach them by rote. For lower elementary students who read, consider using a word visual with designated "special" words. When teaching "special" words, prepare each by having the children perform the rhythm on a level of body percussion before transferring it to instruments.

Suggestion for instruments:

→	=	Glissando on barred instruments, upward
←	=	Glissando on barred instruments, downward
/////	=	Triangle
~~	=	Temple blocks
◯	=	Vibraslap
X X X	=	Tambourine
☁	=	Hand drum

Using Unpitched Percussion Instruments

ACTIVITIES

Hey Diddle Diddle,
The cat and the fiddle,
The cow jumped over the moon.
The little dog laughed, to see such sport,
And the dish ran away with the spoon.

Designate each underlined noun as a level of body percussion or a gesture. After all children can speak the poem rhythmically with the levels of body percussion, transfer each noun to a different unpitched instrument.

Suggestions for instruments:

cat	=	Finger cymbals
cow	=	Cow bell
moon	=	Suspended cymbal
dog	=	Sleigh bells
spoon	=	Triangle

After adding all instruments, see if the children can internalize the words and use only unpitched percussion instruments for the nouns, in the appropriate places.

Using Unpitched and Barred Instruments

ACTIVITIES

STAR LIGHT, STAR BRIGHT

New York

Star light, star bright, first star I see to-night, I wish I may, I

wish I might have the wish I wish to-night.

BORDUN:
Bass Metallophone

Suggestions for teaching: After the children have learned the song, ask them to sing while patting knees using the rhythm of the bordun accompaniment. Select some children to play the bordun on bass instruments. Sing the song and add finger snaps for the word "star"; transfer the snaps to a triangle. Sing the song again and add a clap for the word "wish." Transfer this to the metallophones, which have been put into F pentatonic (B's and E's removed). Encourage the children playing metallophones to play any two notes on the word "wish," changing notes each time.

(The success in adding instruments depends upon the preparation. *Each instrumental part should be prepared rhythmically, and each part should be prepared singly.*)

OLD MOTHER BROWN

Folk Song

Old Moth-er Brown went to town, Rid - ing on a po - ny. When she came back She

took off her hat and gave it to Miss Mac - ro - ni.

Sleigh Bells:

BORDUN: Bass Xylophone

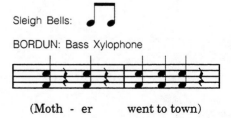

(Moth - er went to town)

Suggestions for teaching: Create an A₁ Section by transferring the rhythm of measures 1 and 2 of the melody to a tambourine; measures 3 and 4 to temple blocks; measures 5 and 6 to a slit drum; measures 7 and 8 to a hand drum.

HAMMER RING

Georgia

Don't you hear the ham-mer ring-ing? Ham-mer ring, Ham-mer ring? Ham-mer ring, Ham-mer ring?

BORDUN:
Bass Xylophone

Suggestions for teaching: Create an A₁ Section for unpitched percussion. For example:

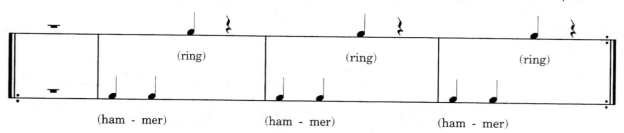

(ring)   (ring)   (ring)

(ham - mer)   (ham - mer)   (ham - mer)

A BIG TURTLE

Konnie Saliba

A   great   big   tur - tle,   sit - ting   on   a   log,

Watch - ing   a   tad - pole   turn   in - to   a   frog.

BORDUN: Bass Xylophone

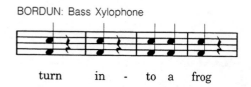

turn   in - to   a   frog

Suggestions for teaching:

Add gestures and eliminate words, two measures at a time.

Eliminate: "A great big turtle."

Substitute: showing, in the air, a large circle with both arms.

At the next repeat of the song, eliminate: "Sitting on a log."

Substitute: the imitation of gently sitting down.

Eliminate: "Watching a tadpole."

Substitute: encircling both eyes with thumb and forefinger for the word "watching."

Eliminate: "turn into a frog."

Substitute: arms in the air, rotating one around the other.

At the final performance of the song, have the children sing the melody with all the gestures.

2

Middle Elementary Grades

Rhythm

IMITATION

Imitation, sometimes called echo-play, is an important part of rhythmic training. When using this technique, the teacher claps a phrase and it is imitated by the children. Imitation creates an immediate focus for all participants and helps train memory and accuracy. Imitation also provides an important foundation for understanding form.

Imitation should not begin until the child knows phrase length. In lower elementary grades, there should have been many movement, singing, and speech experiences in musical phrases. As a rhythmic structure, the phrase is long enough to allow for tension and relaxation.

Meters for imitation should begin with 2/₄ (four measures) or 3/₄ (also four measures). Dynamic variation can occur from the beginning.

Imitation makes immediate use of body percussion. Four levels are possible:

Finger snapping (soprano level)
Clapping hands (alto level)
Patting knees (tenor level)
Stamping feet (bass level)

When the levels are notated on a rhythmic score, the following abbreviations are used:

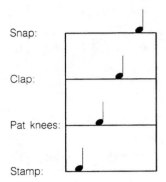

It is best to begin with clapping and with note values of ♩, ♫, and ♩ ♪ (♩). For example:

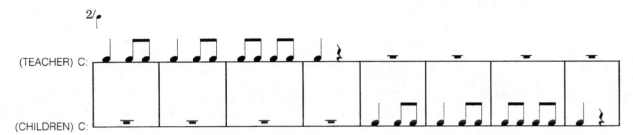

The following is a list of suggestions for first experiences with imitation exercises.

1. Begin with clapping.
2. Add dynamics.
3. Use rhythms that fall on the pulse (convergent).
4. Do not repeat patterns with the children.
5. Repeat a pattern that is not imitated accurately.
6. Include some phrases on another level (snapping, patting, or stamping).
7. Leave a rest at the end of each rhythmic phrase so that the children know where to begin their imitation.

Rhythms for Imitation on One Level

As skill levels increase, provide examples that use two levels of body percussion.

Rhythms for Imitation on Two Levels

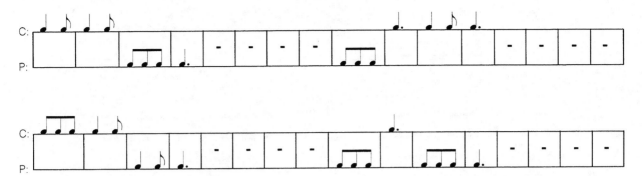

As skill levels continue to increase, include examples that use the note values of ♪♪♪♪, ♪♪♪, and ♪♪♪.

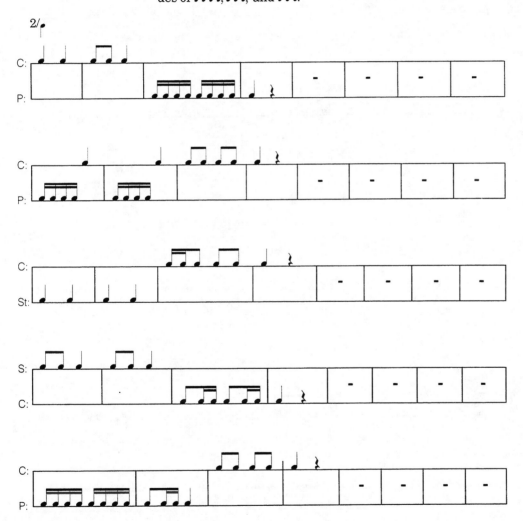

OSTINATO

The ostinato is a pattern, repeated at least once, that in Orff-Schulwerk is used as an accompaniment. Ostinati are excellent devices for rhythmic and melodic training because they can be taught to everyone, and music making can occur almost immediately. The ostinato can be rhythmic, melodic, or harmonic; it can be performed verbally, vocally, instrumentally, or in movement.

Verbal Ostinati

ACTIVITIES

TEXT

You'll ne-ver see flies a-round our place. And ve-ry few bee-tles or bugs. I

should-n't say this, but I will an-y-way, We sweep them all un-der our rugs.

OSTINATO 1

Bzzt   Bzzt   Bzzt Bzzt Bzzt

OSTINATO 2

Step on him!   Get him!

"Now Are You Sure?" from *If Zoos Were Full of Kangaroos* by Edna Snyder John.
Copyright 1975 by Edna John. Used by permission.

Divide the class into three groups. One-third speak the poem, one-third speak ostinato 1, and one-third speak ostinato 2. Switch parts so that all the children have an opportunity to perform each part.

TEXT

Chook, chook, chook, chook, chook. Good morn-ing Mis-sus Hen. How ma-ny chick-ens

have you got? Ma-dam, I've got ten. Four of them are yel-low, and four of them are

brown. And two of them are speck-led red, The nic-est in the town.

OSTINATO

Chook,   chook,   chook, chook, chook!

Be certain to encourage varied vocal inflection for the ostinato. Ask someone in the class to create an introduction and a coda using the word "chook."

Body Percussion Ostinato

The easiest ostinato for body percussion is one in two levels, choosing among clapping, patting knees, and snapping. Using the stamp is always more difficult because a stamp is a weight change.

ACTIVITIES

2/♩

TEXT

Ro - ber - ta made the   cus - tard,   She   made   it   real - ly   thick.   And

when   her   friends   had   lunch   with   her,   It   made   them   ve - ry   sick!

OSTINATO

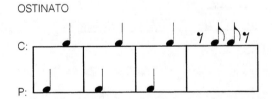

C:

P:

Have the children create an introduction and a coda from the following speech patterns by layering them one at a time.

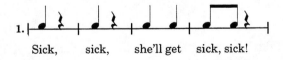

1.

Sick,   sick,   she'll get sick, sick!

2.

Mix the cus-tard, mix the cus-tard, make it good and thick.   Yuk Yuk

3.

Ro - ber - ta,   Ro - ber - ta.

TEXT

You'll pro-ba-bly think I'm tell-ing the truth But I'm not, I'm tell-ing a fib.

This is my name, Be - lieve it or not, Mc - Dib-ble, Mc - Dab-ble, Mc - Dib.

OSTINATO

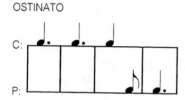

"The Fibber," from *If Zoos Were Full of Kangaroos* by Edna Snyder John.
Copyright 1975 by Edna John. Used by permission.

Create a coda by dividing the class into two groups. Have them speak the following words, first as *forte* speech, then as *piano* speech.

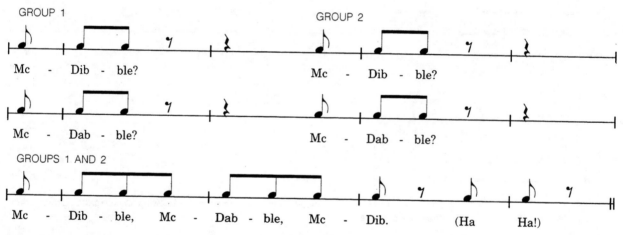

GROUP 1

Mc - Dib - ble?

Mc - Dab - ble?

GROUP 2

Mc - Dib - ble?

Mc - Dab - ble?

GROUPS 1 AND 2

Mc - Dib - ble, Mc - Dab - ble, Mc - Dib. (Ha Ha!)

READING GAMES

When children can read (around the age of seven), you may introduce note values to them. If lower elementary students have had many experiences with such things as the goose, the duck, and chickies (as explained in Chapter 1), then they will have no trouble transferring those experiences to an abstraction, or notation. Because performing sixteenth notes requires a higher level of motor skill, begin reading experiences with only the half note, the quarter note, and the eighth note.

toe   ta   tee - tee (tee-ree-tee-ree)

ACTIVITIES

Divide the class into three groups. Have one group speak the half note (*toe*), one the quarter note (*ta*), and one the eighth notes (*tee-tee*). Indicate, by pointing, which group or groups are to speak. Encourage different voice levels.

Using the same visualization:

a. Perform the rhythmic exercise on body percussion.

　　♩ = Pat knees.

　　♩ = Clap.

　　♫ = Snap.

b. Perform the rhythmic exercise on unpitched percussion instruments.

　　♩ = Metals

　　♩ = Hand drums

　　♫ = Woods

c. Perform the rhythmic exercise on barred instruments in C pentatonic (F's and B's removed).

　　♩ = Metallophones

　　. = Xylophones

　　♫ = Glockenspiels

d. When some children are ready, add the sixteenth-note value. Perform the rhythmic exercise on barred instruments, leaving all bars in. Allow a student to be the conductor and indicate to the groups who is to play while you improvise at the piano, using black keys. The musical result will sound aleatoric.

　　♩ = Metallophones, gong, cymbal

　　♩ = Glockenspiels

　　♫ = Xylophones

　　♬ = Woods and bongos

Choose some children's names to notate and have the children create a rhythmic phrase. For example:

Chris-to-pher   Ri - ley,   Ma - ry Sue   Boyd,   Jen - ni - fer Gri - san - ti,   Jim - my   Beam.

Create an ensemble experience by adding a pulse accompaniment on timpani, speaking the names and then transferring the rhythm to selected unpitched percussion instruments.

When children are beat-competent, they should be encouraged to perform rhythm. This also means that a rhythm, whether it be a grouping of names or a rhyme, can be accompanied by a pulse accompaniment or by an ostinato that falls on the pulse. For example:

TRANSFERRING THE RHYTHM OF WORDS TO INSTRUMENTS

6/₈ There was a man in our town,
And he was wondrous wise,
He <u>jumped</u> into a quickset hedge,
And <u>scratched</u> out both his eyes.

And when he saw his eyes were out,
With all his might and main
He <u>jumped</u> into another hedge,
And <u>scratched</u> them in again.

Have the children do the following: Speak the nursery rhyme in a 6/₈ meter. When the rhythm is secure, speak the words and clap each syllable. Next eliminate speaking, and just clap each syllable. Transfer the rhythm of the words to hand drums. While some children play the rhythm on hand drums, others in the class stamp for the word "jumped" and clap for "scratched." Transfer "jumped" to a vibraslap, "scratched" to the guiro and the cabaza. Add an ostinato on the timpani: ♩. ♪ ♩. ♪ ♩ ♩ ♩ ♪.. Create a form. For example:

> Introduction: timpani
> Speech with timpani
> Unpitched percussion with timpani
> Coda: timpani

Isolating Some Words, Transferred to Instruments

2/₄ A <u>horse</u> and a flea and three blind mice,

Sat on a curbstone shooting dice.

The horse he slipped and fell on the flea.

The flea said, "Whoops! There's a <u>horse</u> on me."

Have the children speak the nursery rhyme in 2/₄ meter. When the rhythm is secure, have them speak and add a different level of body percussion for each special word. Eliminate speaking and transfer the special word or words to instruments. For example:

<u>horse</u> = Vibraslap

flea = Finger cymbals

three blind mice = Temple blocks

"Whoops! There's a <u>horse</u> on me" = Drums

Create a form. For example: Perform the poem three times using

Speech only
Body percussion only
Unpitched percussion only

Melody

WAYS TO WORK WITH MELODIC READING

Before the children can read music, they must be certain of the meanings of high and low. Children frequently relate high to loud and low to soft. To eliminate confusion, work on this concept should begin with the preschool-aged child, and it should be extended into multiple activities leading toward note reading.

ACTIVITIES

Play clusters of tones on the piano, first in the high register of the instrument, then in the low. Ask the children to show with their arms in the air whether they hear high or low tones. Gradually diminish the range so that the tones are closer together. From tones on the piano, arrive at C'–A (Sol–Mi).

Use Curwen hand signs[1] for echo singing.

Have the children sing melodies as you point to patterns on a syllable ladder.

Remove all the bars from a glockenspiel except for C' and A. Turn the glockenspiel lengthwise against a chalkboard so that children can see that C is higher than A.

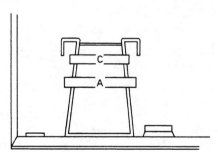

With the glockenspiel in the lengthwise position, play patterns on C and A for the children to echo-sing.

Extend the lines on the chalkboard, using the glockenspiel bars as a guide for lines and spaces. Using the chalk on the metal bars, play a pattern; write the pattern in the spaces. Repeat this game many times, and use this visualization to introduce new notes.

[1]For the Curwen hand signs, see the Appendix.

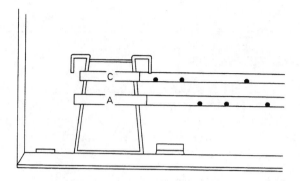

Place felt pictures on a flannel board to teach a three- or four-note melody. For example:

Ask the class to listen to a melody, such as the following one, as you sing or play it on the recorder. Before the children listen a second time, ask them to raise their hands each time they hear a Sol-Mi pattern. Ask the children to sing the Sol-Mi pattern each time it occurs, or to play it on barred instruments.

CUCKOO

Konnie Saliba

Cuck - oo,   cuck - oo,   Don't   try   to   hide   from

me.   Cuck - oo,   cuck - oo,   I   see   you   in   the   tree.

Display a note visual showing the C-to-A interval.

THE PENTATONIC SCALE

Children who are schooled in the Orff-Schulwerk approach develop an understanding of melody and intervallic relationships through a careful exploration of pentatonic scales. Through varied experiences, the child is allowed many opportunities to sing and play in this tension-free atmosphere of sound. The pentatonic scale used in Orff-Schulwerk is particularly apropos for improvisation experiences.

By definition, a pentatonic scale is a scale with five different tones. The pentatonic scale used in Orff-Schulwerk is based upon two cells, the first at the dominant, with a tone above and one below—the universally known "childhood chant."

Melodies around the dominant are open in sound and never have a final ending. The second cell functions at the tonic, moving in whole steps.

Some not familiar with the Orff-Schulwerk approach might wonder at the reasoning for the melodic progression to the pentatonic. For the child, the pentatonic offers a tension-free environment of sound because of the absence of half steps. The open fifth, bordun accompaniment is always possible, so that many melodies can be beautifully and simply accompanied by the children themselves. The absence of half steps also allows all tones to sound together, meaning that children can begin experience with improvisation early in their musical training. This offers a real opportunity for each child to express himself or herself creatively. The pentatonic is universal. All cultures of the world, and especially the American culture, have pentatonic melodies.

For singing, the preferred pentatonic scale is F because it is high enough to encourage a light, head-tone singing sound, but not too high to be above a child's optimum vocal range.

F PENTATONIC SCALE

ACTIVITIES

MISTER RABBIT

American Folk Song

Mis - ter Rab - bit, Mis - ter Rab - bit, your tail's might - y white.

Yes, bless God, been get - tin' out - a sight. ___

Ev - 'ry lit - tle soul gwine - a shine, shine. ___

Ev - 'ry lit - tle soul gwine - a shine a - long.

BORDUN: Bass Xylophone and Bass Metallophone

⁺At each sign, ask some children to play any two notes in F pentatonic on soprano and alto metallophones, changing notes each time.

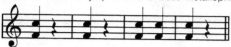

Add a movement game. Ask the children to move freely in the space during the first eight measures, finding a partner by measure 9. The following hand-clap game can be played with a partner.

Clap both partner's hands:

Clap left hand with partner:

Clap right hand with partner:

Clap own hands:

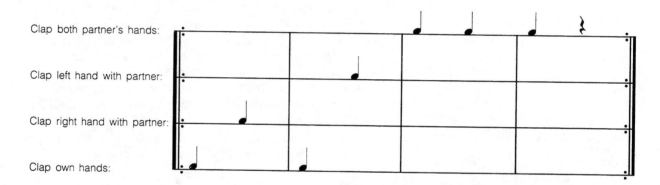

HEY, CHILDREN, WHO'S IN TOWN?

Konnie Saliba

Hey, child - ren, who's in town? Ev - 'ry - bo - dy stop and look a - round.

Hey, child - ren, who's in town? Tell us your name and then sit down.

BORDUN: Bass Xylophone

Ask the entire class to stand while singing the song the first time. Make a B Section, using four first and last names of class participants. Ask each person who speaks his or her name to do so "creatively"—that is, using a high voice, a low voice, or a staccato voice, or combining speech with movement, and then sit down.

Variations: Each child may speak his or her name and then play it on an unpitched percussion instrument or on a barred instrument in F pentatonic (B's and E's removed).

RAIN, COME WET ME

American Folk Song

Rain, come wet me. Sun, come dry me. Keep a - way, pret-ty girls, don't come nigh me.

Make two melodic visuals that the class can watch as you sing or play the melody on the recorder. Ask children in the class to sequence the visuals into the melody.

Ask some children in the class to play any two notes in F pentatonic (B's and E's removed) on soprano and alto metallophones on each underlined word.

THE CLOCK STORE

Konnie Saliba

1. I went to the clock store and what did I see? A grand - fa - ther clock,*

smil - ing at me. I went to the clock store and heard a lit - tle bird. I

lis - tened to Grand - fa - ther clock and this is what I heard.

BORDUN:
Bass Xylophone

*Verses:
2. A grandmother clock . . .
3. A little cuckoo clock . . .
4. A store full of clocks . . .

Add these verses: a grandmother clock, a little cuckoo clock, and a store full of clocks. After singing verse 1, select a child to represent the grandfather clock by playing the wood block (♩ 𝄽). Grandmother clock may be a two-toned wood block (♩ ♩), and the little cuckoo clock may be the claves (♫ ♫). For the last verse, have all three instruments play simultaneously.

I KNOW JUST WHAT I'LL DO

Konnie Saliba

The   first thing in   the   morn-ing when   I   get   out   of   bed,   I

stand   up   straight   and   I   shake   my   head.   I

lis - ten   to   the   bird - ies sing "Good morn - ing   to   you."   And

then   I   know   ex - act - ly   what   I   shall   do.

BORDUN: Bass Xylophone

Create an improvised introduction of the "woods at sunrise" with the barred instruments in F pentatonic (B's and E's removed) and selected unpitched percussion instruments such as a cabaza, a wood block, and wind chimes. Those playing barred instruments may tremolo softly on any two notes. Add unpitched percussion sounds randomly.

After singing verse 1, a small group of children may improvise for the length of a verse on selected unpitched percussion instruments, or the entire class may improvise using body percussion.

F PENTACHORD

Adding the fourth scale degree to a major pentatonic scale creates a pentachord. Melodies are easy to sing because of the stepwise progression.

ACTIVITIES

MORNINGS ARE FOR SINGING

Konnie Saliba

Morn - ings   are   for   sing - ing,   Morn - ings   are   for   fun.

Let's be - gin the morn - ing by sing - ing one by one.

BORDUN: Bass Xylophone

Add a B Section, using four children from the class who individually sing their names on the falling third (C'–A). Or after a name is sung, it could be played on a glockenspiel using the high C to A.

MICKEY MOUSE

Konnie Saliba

Mic - key Mouse built a house, un - der an ap - ple tree.

Mic - key Mouse called his house num - ber twen - ty three.

BORDUN: Bass Xylophone

With each repeat of the song, eliminate singing a measure and substitute gestures such as those listed here.

Mickey Mouse	=	Show "mouse ears" on top of the head on beat 1, "mouse whiskers" on beat 4.
built a house	=	In the air, show the roof and sides of the house on beats 1 and 4.
under an apple	=	Indicate with body the word "under."
tree	=	Show a large tree with arms and entire body.
called his house	=	Cup hands to mouth.
number twenty	=	Clap each syllable.
three	=	Stamp.

I SAW THREE SHIPS

Konnie Saliba

I saw a ship a - sail - ing, a - sail - ing on the sea. I

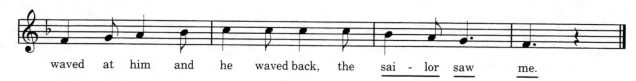

waved   at   him   and   he   waved back,   the   sai - lor   saw   me.

BORDUN: Bass Xylophone

Create an A₁ Section, and an inner-ear exercise, by eliminating singing, and, instead, playing the underlined words on selected unpitched percussion instruments in the 6/8 pulse.

IT'S AS EASY AS CAN BE

Konnie Saliba

Join   with   me,   you   will   see,   It's   as   ea - sy   as   can   be.

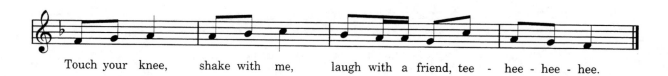

Touch   your   knee,   shake with   me,   laugh   with   a   friend, tee - hee - hee - hee.

Divide the class into partners and add the following movement:

Measures 1–4:   Partners hook elbows and make a single circle, skipping.

Measures 5–8:   Add gestures as the words indicate.

Add a B Section (see the following example) in an additive manner, two measures at a time. That is, sing the song once, and for B add only measures 1 and 2; repeat the song and add measures 1, 2, 3, and 4; and so on.

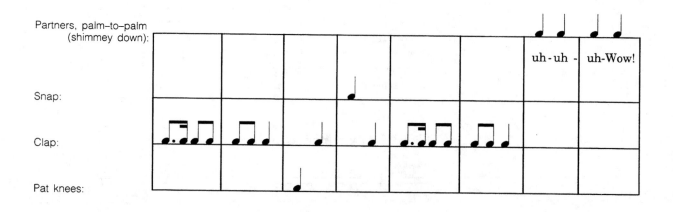

Movement

The young child who sings also moves. The child who plays also sings and moves. Movement is integral to a child's waking hours. Any child below the age of ten years anxiously awaits recess and the end of the school day to be with friends and move and play. Yet, during the school day, almost all opportunities for movement are eliminated. Quiet in the halls and orderliness while walking to and from classes are the norm for an efficiently run school.

Since 1979, music educators have heard many reasons why children should be allowed to move. We know that movement helps integrate rhythm and melody and that being allowed to move relieves stress and tension created by sedentary activities. But in reality, many music specialists do not include movement in their teaching. Reasons given include, "There is not enough space in my classroom," and, "I only see my classes twice a week, and there are so many other things to do." Although those reasons are valid, if the truth were known, the teacher probably does not include movement because he or she feels inadequate in this area and is afraid of losing control of the class.

The ideas presented in this chapter are not in the form of a continuum of movement training, nor do they give all the kinds of examples possible. For that, the music specialist must seek training in the combination of music and movement. The ideas presented here have a structure. The author hopes that that structure will encourage any music teacher to move the chairs to the outer edges of the room to provide opportunities for the children to explore some of these movement possibilities. Many of the activities are extensions of those presented for lower elementary children. But the primary difference in locomotor exercises for middle elementary children is that they require the children to step to a beat, a prerequisite to adding movement forms to songs.

It is the author's belief that any attempts to include movement in music classes, if done honestly and with regularity, will result in improvements in coordination, the playing of instruments, self-satisfaction, and concentration.

LOCOMOTION AND PHRASE BUILDING

ACTIVITIES

Have the children walk forward with the sound of the low drum (an 8-beat phrase) and freeze into place with the sound of the high drum.

Variations: Let the children freeze into shapes such as a snowman, a statue, a rabbit, and so on.

Have the children listen to an 8-beat phrase as it is being played on the drum, then move.

Variation: Change the tempo.

Have the children walk in space, keeping a quarter-note pulse in the feet. When you give a number signal (a number between 1 and 10), each child should place that number of body parts on the floor. For example, if the signal were 1, each child would stand on one foot; the signal 3 might be both feet and an elbow.

Variation: Divide the class into partners. On a number signal, the partners have to decide which parts of their bodies, in combination, touch the floor.

With the drum playing the pulse, have the children walk an 8-beat phrase, then walk 7 beats and internalize 1 beat; walk 6 and internalize 2; walk 5 and internalize 3; and so on. Reverse the process, beginning with one internalized beat and seven walking steps.

Have the children run for 8 beats, and stop for 8.

Combine phrases of movement using a walk, a run, and a skip.

Improvise, in 8-beat phrases, at the piano. When the children hear the low register, they move appropriately in space. When they hear the high register, they use nonlocomotor movement, with the feet stationary.

Explore direction: The children move forward when hearing a phrase being played on the drum. They move in another direction, or make a floor pattern such as a circle, a diagonal, or a zigzag, when hearing a phrase being played on a wood block.

Explore level: Have the children move in phrases and allow their bodies to move high in the air or low to the ground or in combinations.

Use a poem and vary the movement activities. For example:

3/₄   Handy Pandy, Jack-a-dandy
       Loves plum cake
       And sugar candy.

Ask the children to speak the poem while standing in place and then to internalize the words and walk in space for the length of the poem.

Variation: Change the locomotion to skipping, running, hopping, or jumping.

ACCENTS IN 2/₄ METER

ACTIVITIES

1. Have the children listen to the accents you play on a hand drum: $\overset{>}{}\overset{>}{}$. Ask the children to do such activities as these:

    a. Clap on the accent.
    b. Clap and move with the accent.
    c. Show the accent in movement with strong and weak steps.
    d. Play the accent on an unpitched instrument.
    e. Play and move with the accent.
    f. Play the accent and move on the weak beat.

2. Use a rhyme in 2/₄ meter.

    Sticks and stones will break my bones,

    But names will never hurt me.

    When I die, then you'll cry,

    For the names you've called me.

Have the children do the following:

    a. Speak the poem and show the accents in movement.
    b. Clap and move with the accents.
    c. Show accents in movement, first on the left foot and then on the right foot.

PHRASES IN 6/₈ METER

ACTIVITIES

Ask the children to listen to phrases they hear being played on a drum. Have them walk if they hear accents in 2/₄ and skip with the 6/₈. For example:

Use a rhyme in 6/₈ meter. Ask the children to notice the lilting feeling of the 6/₈ in contrast to the marchlike quality of 2/₄.

Humpty Dumpty sat on a wall.

Humpty Dumpty had a great fall.

All the king's horses, and all the king's men,

Couldn't put Humpty together again.

Have the children do the following:

    a. Speak the poem while doing a lilting step in the feet, stopping on the last word.

    b. Speak the poem and skip.

    c. Speak the poem; internalize the words and skip afterwards, stopping on the last word.

    d. One-half of the class clap each accent and one-half move; switch groups.

CIRCLES

ACTIVITIES

Let the children move anywhere in the room with the sound of the low drum. Have them make a continuously moving circle with the sound of the high drum.

Let the children skip anywhere in space when they hear the rhythm ♩♪♩♪, and form one continuously moving circle when they hear ♩♩♩♩.

In a circle formation, sing a familiar song (A). Ask the children to internalize the words and, during this time, move freely in space (B), returning to the circle by the last measure of the internalized melody. (This exercise is fun for children but will need to be repeated many times, with variations.)

Have the children move clockwise or counterclockwise in a circle, matching feet to a drum pulse. When they hear a phrase on a wood block, they should bend different parts of the body with feet stationary. When they hear the sleigh bells, they should shake one or more parts of the body with feet stationary.

Experiment with different things that can be done in a circle formation.

    a. Moving counterclockwise

    b. Moving clockwise

    c. Moving forward, counterclockwise, and backward, clockwise

    d. Moving in to the center and back out

    e. Moving clockwise with quarter notes in the feet and counterclockwise with half notes in the feet

    f. Moving into the center with quarter notes in the feet and out with half notes in the feet

Sing a song, in a circle formation. Let the children decide upon a way the circle can move for the A Section and different nonlocomotor movements that might occur for the B Section.

PUT THE BEAT IN YOUR FEET

Konnie Saliba

A SECTION

Let us sing and move our feet, La la, la, la, la, la, la. La, la, la, la, la.
Put the beat right in your feet,

B SECTION (Speech)

Shake, shake, shake your hands, shake them high, shake them low.

Shake, shake, shake your hands, Make a cir - cle and 'round you go.

The movement for the following song is done in a circle formation.

CIRCLE SONG

Konnie Saliba

A SECTION

We are in a cir - cle, cir - cle, cir - cle.

We are in a cir - cle hold - ing hands.
touch - ing elbows.
touch - ing shoulders.
hold - ing waists.
touch - ing knees.
touch - ing ankles.

Lie, lie, *etc.*

The A Section is sung with no movement. The B Section always has locomotor movement—a slide-close movement, eight measures in a counterclockwise direction and eight measures in a clockwise direction—"holding hands" as verse 1 indicates. Add verses, such as those suggested.

B SECTION

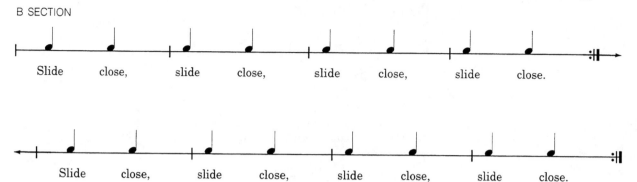

Slide   close,   slide   close,   slide   close,   slide   close.

Slide   close,   slide   close,   slide   close,   slide   close.

NONLOCOMOTOR MOVEMENT

The following song may be sung in a circle formation, in lines, or with children freely spaced in the room. Do many verses.

I SHAKE MY THUMB

Traditional

I shake my thumb, la, la, la, la, la. I shake my thumb, ha, ha, ha,

ha. I shake my thumb, la, la, la, la, la. I shake my thumb, ha, ha, ha, ha.

Verses: 2. I shake the other
3. I shake them both
4. I shake my arm
5. I shake the other
6. I shake them both
7. I shake my foot
8. I shake the other
9. I shake them both
10. I shake my leg
11. I shake the other
12. I shake them both
13. I shake everything

LINES

ACTIVITIES

1. Ask each child to listen to the following pattern and add two snaps for the rests at the end of the phrase.

(snap snap)

2. Ask some children to skip in the space and stop for the snaps; ask all children to skip with the rhythm and stop for the snaps.

3. Ask the children to use a side gallop instead of a skip, with a change of direction after the snap.

4. Try activity 3 with half a phrase.

(snap snap)

5. Add words:

Halloween, it's Halloween, it's Halloween tonight.
Halloween, it's Halloween, it's Halloween tonight.
Witches fly up high,
Ghosts are in the sky.
Goblins make a special sound,
Aiee, Aiee, Aiee!

6. The movement form for the poem can be done in lines, with children facing one another, the two lines moving in the same direction.

7. **Variations:** Transfer words to wood, unpitched percussion instruments; transfer ♪ ♩. to hand drums.

Use the folk song "I Hear the Train A-Coming" for a movement-in-lines experience, as a train might move at different speeds.

ACTIVITIES

I HEAR THE TRAIN A-COMING

Georgia Folk Song

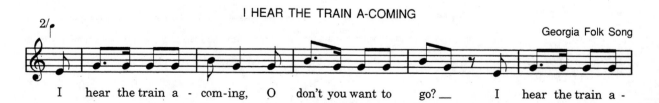

I   hear the train a - com-ing,   O   don't you want to   go? ___   I   hear the train a -

com-ing, O don't you want to go? ___ I hear the train a - com-ing, O

don't you want to go? ___ Oh ____ yes, I want to go.

Ask the children to form one or more lines, each line being a train. Each child places the left hand on the shoulder of the person in front; the right hand moves in a pulse of a half note, the same pulse as is in the feet.

Variations: Have the children sing the song with a quarter-note pulse in the feet and the right hand; sing with an eighth-note pulse.

PARTNERS AND CHANGING PARTNERS

ACTIVITIES

MINNIE

Konnie Saliba

Min-nie and a Min-nie and a ha, ha, ha. Kissed her fel - la on a broad-way car.

You tell Ma and I'll tell Pa, Min-nie and a Min-nie and a ha, ha, ha.

Ask the children to choose partners and space themselves freely in the room. Add the following pulse game for body percussion. During measures 5 and 6, one person in each pair runs around his or her partner, returning to repeat the game.

Variation: During measures 5 and 6, partners separate, finding a new partner by measure 7.

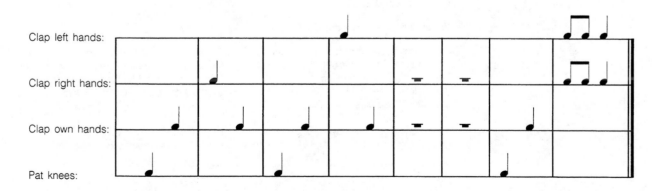

Poem

One, two, three, four, five.

I caught a fish alive.

Six, seven, eight, nine, ten.

Then I let him go again.

Ask the children to choose partners and space themselves freely in the room. Create a body percussion pulse game to be used while speaking the words. For an A_1 Section, ask the children to internalize the words, putting the numbers in their feet. During the internalized section, each child should move in space and find a new partner by the last word of the poem so that the game can be repeated.

CREATIVE MOVEMENT

ACTIVITIES

Create a "walking dance." Each child is walking somewhere—perhaps, the woods or the fair or downtown. Each time the music stops, everyone "freezes" for a moment. When the music begins again, there is something new to see, another way to walk, and another direction to take. Explore direction level, intensity, and tempo.

Create a "running story." Each child is in a forest. Each child must run to get out of the forest, but with frequent stops. There are branches, trees, and streams that must be avoided.

Ask each child to choose someone across the room from him or her and walk toward that person in slow motion. When the partners reach one another, they move together in slow motion.

Use streamers or scarves and try some of the following activities:

    a. With feet in place, make the streamers fly sometimes high, sometimes low.
    b. Move into space, making the streamers fly high.
    c. Make a shape with the streamers in the air.
    d. Move with a partner; see if the partner can run under the streamers.
    e. Select three or four movements with streamers and create a dance.
    f. Show very strong and very light movements with the streamers.

Use a poem, such as the following one, to encourage improvised solo or small-group movement.

Wicked, wicked witches
Stealing through the night.
Show us how you'll move
On Halloween night.

Variations: Use ghosts, goblins, or black cats.

Explore mirror movement: A movement is created by one person and imitated simultaneously, with sides reversed, by another. Children should be encouraged to move slowly and have direct eye contact with their partners. Before children work in partners, it is advisable that the teacher be the model in order to explore facial expression, isolation of body parts, and levels. It is helpful to use music that is quiet and slow.

The following creative movement game can be done with the entire class, in partners, or in small groups. Ask the children to show, in movement, what they think the abstraction looks like.

Variation: Sequence two or more movements, and see if class members can choose the correct visuals for the movement they see.

Using Orff Instruments

REACTION EXERCISES AND TIMBRE EXPERIENCES

With all barred instruments in C pentatonic (F's and B's removed), have the children do the following activities.

Play any two notes as the teacher conducts a downbeat, changing notes with each new downbeat.

Using alternation of hands, create a melody from a phrase of rhythm clapped by the teacher.

Relate the four levels of body percussion to the barred instruments.

Snapping	=	Soprano and alto glockenspiels
Clapping	=	Soprano xylophone and soprano metallophone
Patting knees	=	Alto xylophone and alto metallophone
Stamping	=	Bass xylophone and bass metallophone

If the teacher claps a pattern, only the soprano xylophone and metallophone create a melody using the rhythm; if the teacher pats knees in a rhythmic pattern, only the alto instruments create the melody; and so on.

As the teacher, create rhythmic patterns on two levels. For example:

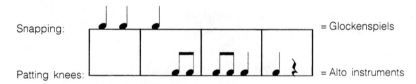

Relate the four levels of body percussion to the unpitched percussion instruments.

Snapping	=	Metals (triangle, sleigh bells, etc.)
Clapping	=	Woods (claves, wood blocks, etc.)
Patting knees	=	Membranes (hand drums)
Stamping	=	Big percussion (bass drum, gong, etc.)

USING UNPITCHED PERCUSSION INSTRUMENTS: CUMULATIVE WITH A SONG

ACTIVITIES

GOING TO THE FARM

Konnie Saliba

We're go-ing to the farm to - day.   We're go-ing to the farm to - day.   To

find some an - i - mals that we all like,   to come a - long and join our hike,   We're

go-ing to the farm to - day.   We're go-ing to the farm to - day.

Sheep	goes,	Baa.
Cow	goes,	Moo.
Dog	goes,	Bow wow.
Cat	goes,	Meow.
Duck	goes,	Quack.
Pig	goes,	Oink.
Donkey	goes,	Hee haw.
Rooster	goes,	
	Cock-a-doodle,	
	cock-a-doodle doo.	

BORDUN: Bass Xylophone

With the children's help, select an appropriate-sounding unpitched percussion instrument for each of the animals in the song. Sing the melody and add the sheep. Repeat the melody and sing the cow, followed by the sheep (in reverse order), and so on.

Variation: Eliminate singing the sound each animal makes, and use only the unpitched percussion instrument.

TRANSFERRING THE RHYTHM OF WORDS TO UNPITCHED PERCUSSION INSTRUMENTS

Transferring Each LIne of a Poem

ACTIVITIES

Poem

6/8   Witches ride switches across the sky.

Black cats walk quietly by.

The wind in the trees rustles and dies,

And the ghost flies high!

After the rhythm of the poem is secure through varied rhythmic vocal repetitions, ask the children to transfer each line to a level of body percussion: snapping, clapping, patting, or stamping each syllable. Transfer each line to a different unpitched percussion instrument. Suggestions:

Line 1 = Claves
Line 2 = Bass drum
Line 3 = Tambourine
Line 4 = Suspended cymbal

Add an introduction and a coda of sounds in imitation of the wind. **Suggestions:** Include mouth sounds, glissandos on barred instruments, and rubbing the skin of a hand drum.

A Rhythmic Canon Experience

ACTIVITIES

Poem

6/₈ There was a fat man of Bombay,

Who was smoking one sunshiny day;

When a bird called a snipe

Flew away with his pipe,

Which vexed the fat man of Bombay.

After the children have learned the poem, divide the class into two groups, and have them speak in a two-part canon. Begin group 2 after "There was a fat man of." Encourage "interesting" vocal sounds to give the speech canon interest. Ask each child to clap the rhythm of the words while speaking, then without speaking. Try clapping the rhythm of the words in a two-part canon. Transfer the rhythm of the words to drums and wood instruments.

Suggestions for form: Have the class speak the poem in unison. Have only drums play the rhythm of the words; then have only wood instruments play. Last of all, have drums and woods play in a two-part canon.

Adding an Ostinato

ACTIVITIES

Poem

2/₄ | Solomon Grundy, | = All unpitched instruments |
Born on Monday,	= Hand drum
Christened on Tuesday,	= Tambourine
Married on Wednesday,	= Triangle
Took ill on Thursday,	= Guiro
Worse on Friday,	= Suspended cymbal
Died on Saturday,	= Gong
Buried on Sunday,	= Bass drum
This is the end	= Finger cymbals
Of Solomon Grundy.	= All unpitched instruments

Teach the words of the poem with a visual of the words. After the rhythm is secure, have the class clap the rhythm of the words. Transfer each line to an unpitched percussion instrument; suggestions are given above.

Have the children add an ostinato. First pat knees, then transfer the ostinato to two timpani.

OSTINATO

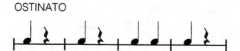

Suggestions for form: Ostinato only (two patterns); speech with ostinato; unpitched percussion without speech, with ostinato.

USING SPEECH FOR INSTRUMENTAL TECHNIQUE

ACTIVITIES

Poem[2]

6/₈ The pickety fence

The pickety fence

Give it a (lick) it's

A clickety fence

Give it a (lick) it's

A lickety fence

Give it a (lick)

Give it a (lick)

Give it a (lick)

With a rickety stick

Pickety

Pickety

Pickety

(Pick)

Use a visual to teach the words. After the rhythm is secure, transfer each syllable of the words that have a wavy line to knee pats. Transfer the circled words to finger snaps. Divide the class. One-half of the class speak and perform the words with wavy lines, the other half the words with circles. Transfer wavy lines to all xylophones that are in C pentatonic (F's and B's removed) and all circles to metallophones and glockenspiels in C pentatonic.

Suggestion for form: Have the class speak the poem in unison, using interesting voices. Ask them to internalize the words and perform the wavy lines and circles on body percussion. Have them internalize the words and transfer body percussion to barred instruments.

Reinforcing the Upbeat

ACTIVITIES

Poem[3]

Bananas and cream

Bananas and cream

All we could say was

Bananas and cream

We couldn't say (fruit)

We wouldn't say cow,

We didn't say (sugar)

We don't say it now

[2]From *One at a Time* by David McCord. "The Pickety Fence" copyright 1952 by David McCord. By permission of Little, Brown and Company.

[3]From *One at a Time* by David McCord. "Bananas and Cream" copyright 1961, 1962 by David McCord. By permission of Little, Brown and Company.

Bananas and cream   We forgot it was (fruit)

Bananas and cream   We forgot the old <u>cow</u>

All we could shout was   We never said (sugar)

Bananas and cream   We only said <u>WOW!</u>

Use a visual to teach the words. After the rhythm is secure, transfer all words with the wavy lines to knee pats. Add the special words in the B and B₁ sections as follows:

fruit   = Hand drum
cow and *now*   = Cow bell
sugar   = Tambourine
WOW   = Vibraslap

Transfer all wavy lines to barred instruments in C pentatonic (F's and B's removed) and all the other "special" words to the unpitched percussion as suggested.

Suggestions for form: Speech and body percussion; internalized words and instruments only.

Adding an Interlude, an Ostinato, and a Coda

ACTIVITIES

Poem

6/₈   Humpty Dumpty sat on the wall,

Humpty Dumpty had a great fall,

All the king's horses and all the king's men,

Couldn't put Humpty together again.

After the rhythm of the words in speech is secure, ask the children to clap each syllable. Transfer this rhythm to temple blocks.

Add an interlude:

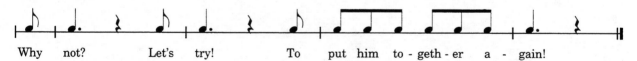

Why   not?   Let's   try!   To   put him to - geth - er   a - gain!

Add parts of the ostinati, one-by-one, as speech interludes before combining them with the poem.

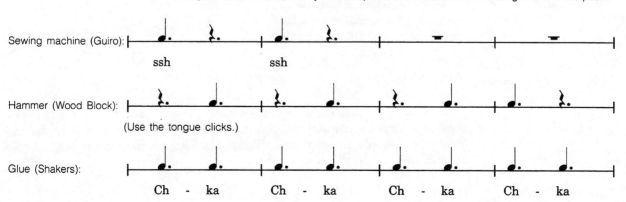

Sewing machine (Guiro):   ssh   ssh

Hammer (Wood Block):

(Use the tongue clicks.)

Glue (Shakers):   Ch - ka   Ch - ka   Ch - ka   Ch - ka

Add the coda:

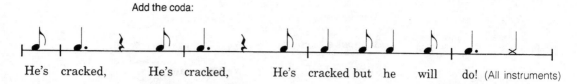

He's cracked,　　He's cracked,　　He's cracked but he will do! (All instruments)

VISUALIZATION OF QUARTER NOTES, EIGHTH NOTES, AND HALF NOTES

Using Quarter-Note, Eighth-Note, and Half-Note Values as Added Sections to a Song

ACTIVITIES

INSTRUMENT SONG

Konnie Saliba

Can you play the　xy - lo - phone,　　xy - lo - phone,　　xy - lo - phone? Show us how it sounds.
　　　　　　　glock-en-spiel,　　glock-en-spiel,　　glock-en-spiel? Show us how it sounds.
　　　　　　　me - tal - lo - phone, me - tal - lo - phone, me - tal - lo - phone? Show us how it sounds.

Make three visuals, one for each note value:

After the children have learned the song, point to the quarter-note visual and ask the children to internalize the words as they pat that pulse on their knees. Transfer that to all xylophone players, who may improvise for the length of the song in F pentatonic (B's and E's removed). Repeat the sequence for glockenspiel players, who improvise using eighth notes, and for metallophone players, who improvise using half notes.

BORDUN: Bass Xylophone

Suggestion for form:

A, Singing; B, Improvisation ♩
A, Singing; C, Improvisation ♫
A, Singing; D, Improvisation ♩
A, Singing

THE SIMPLE BORDUN

The bordun is a harmonization based upon the tonic and the dominant. The tonic is always on the bottom, giving the feeling of a I chord, and is usually played by the bass instruments, so that it is beneath the melody. The simple bordun may be played in four ways:

1. As a chord
2. As a broken chord

3. In levels (octaves of sound)
4. As a crossover (left hand crossing over right)

For lower and middle elementary ages, the best bordun to use is the chord, because the two hands play simultaneously:

As children become sure of their dominant hand, about the age of seven, the broken chord bordun may be introduced in which the left hand plays on all strong beats:

Because a bordun is a *single-harmony accompaniment,* it is suitable for young children as well as being appropriate for many melodies. The bordun can be used with the following:

1. A pentatonic melody (without half steps)
2. A diatonic melody in which all strong beats are notes from the I chord
3. A diatonic melody in which all strong beats are notes from the related pentatonic centers

Chord

Bass Xylophone

ACTIVITIES

GOOD MORNING

Konnie Saliba

Good morn-ing, good morn-ing and how do you do? I'll *shake my head and blink my eyes and

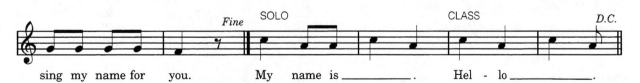

sing my name for you. My name is _____. Hel - lo _____.

Add new verses at the asterisk, such as:

stamp my feet and turn around
touch my nose and touch my toes
pat my knees and pat my head
bend my knees and flap my wings

Broken Chord

Bass Xylophone

ACTIVITIES

HOLD MY MULE

American Folk Song

Hold my mule while   I dance, Jo-sie, Hold my mule while   I dance, Jo-sie   Oh, Miss Su-san Brown.

Create an A₁ Section, based upon the rhythm of the words.

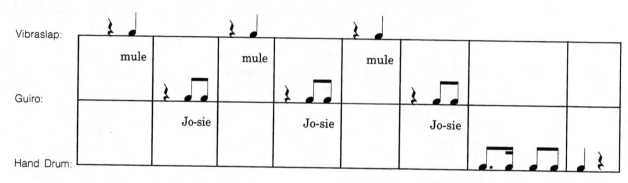

Oh, Miss Su-san Brown

Accompaniments can now be ostinati rather than pulse, and several different instruments can occur in the same orchestration. However, for children at this age, it will still be easier if the ostinati can be linked to the text.

ACTIVITIES

BYE BYE, BABY

Folk Song

Bye   bye, _   ba - by,   ba - by,   bye.   My   lit - tle   ba - by,   ba - by,   bye.

ACCOMPANIMENT
Bass Metallophone

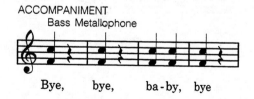

Bye,   bye,   ba - by,   bye

Soprano Metallophone

Ba - by, ba - by, bye

Triangle

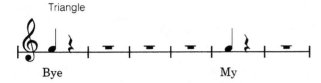

Bye   My

After the children have learned the melody, have them add the parts one-by-one by speaking the rhythms while patting the knees.

CHATTER WITH THE ANGELS

Spiritual

Chat-ter with the an - gels soon in the morn-ing, Chat-ter with the an - gels in that land.
Chat-ter with the an - gels soon in the morn-ing, Chat-ter with the an - gels join that band.

ACCOMPANIMENT
Glockenspiel

soon in the morn-ing

Temple Blocks

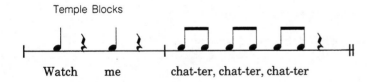

Watch   me   chat-ter, chat-ter, chat-ter

Bass Xylophone

Using speech, add an introduction and a coda to "Chatter with the Angels."

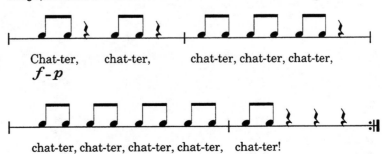

Chat-ter,   chat-ter,   chat-ter, chat-ter, chat-ter,
f - p

chat-ter, chat-ter, chat-ter, chat-ter, chat-ter!

Level

Soprano Metallophone

Alto Metallophone

Bass Metallophone

ACTIVITIES

THE MAN IN THE MOON

Konnie Saliba

The man in the <u>moon</u>, looked out of the <u>moon</u>, looked out of the <u>moon</u> and said, ___ "Tis

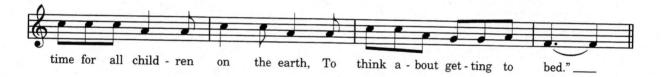

time for all child - ren on the earth, To think a - bout get - ting to bed." ___

Add the suspended cymbal on the underlined word, "moon."

Have the children create a B Section by making a word chain about things that might represent night, such as stars and crickets. Accompany the B Section with tremolos on barred instruments in F pentatonic.

Crossover

Alto Metallophone

BORDUN: Bass Xylophone

L.   R. L.   R.   L.

ACTIVITIES

BIPPETY BOPPETY BOO

Konnie Saliba

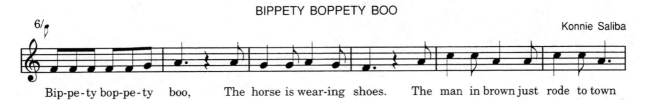

Bip-pe-ty bop-pe-ty   boo,   The horse is wear-ing shoes.   The man in brown just rode to town

Bip-pe-ty bop-pe-ty   boo.

Have the children stand in a circle formation and add the following movement to the melody:

Measures 1–2:	Side-gallop counterclockwise, hands on hips.
Measures 3–4:	Standing in place, "paw" the ground three times with the right foot.
Measures 5–6:	Each child skips in his or her own circle, beginning on the right foot.
Measures 7–8:	Side-gallop clockwise, hands on hips.

Create a game for an A₁ Section. Give a child a hand drum and ask him or her to skip around the outside of the circle while playing the rhythm of the words. On the last word (*boo*), the child stops and gives the hand drum to the child he or she is behind. Then the game can be repeated.

3

Upper Elementary Grades

Rhythm

IMITATION FOR BODY PERCUSSION

Imitation for the upper elementary student serves as one of the ways to improve rhythmic skills. You should spend several minutes of a class period giving rhythmic patterns to be imitated. It is wise to begin with patterns that are not difficult and to gradually increase the difficulty. To increase difficulty, include some of the following:

1. Divergent rhythms—that is, rhythms that do not fall on the pulse, such as ♩.♪; ♩.♪; ♪♩♪; ♫♪
2. Patterns in three or four levels (snapping, clapping, patting knees, stamping)
3. The meter of 3/♪
4. Patterns in different meters—for example, four patterns in 2/♪ followed by four patterns in 6/♪

Rhythms for Imitation

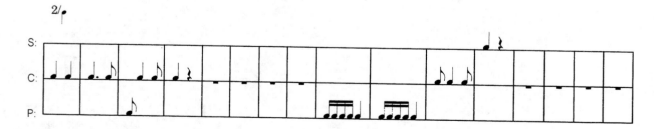

66

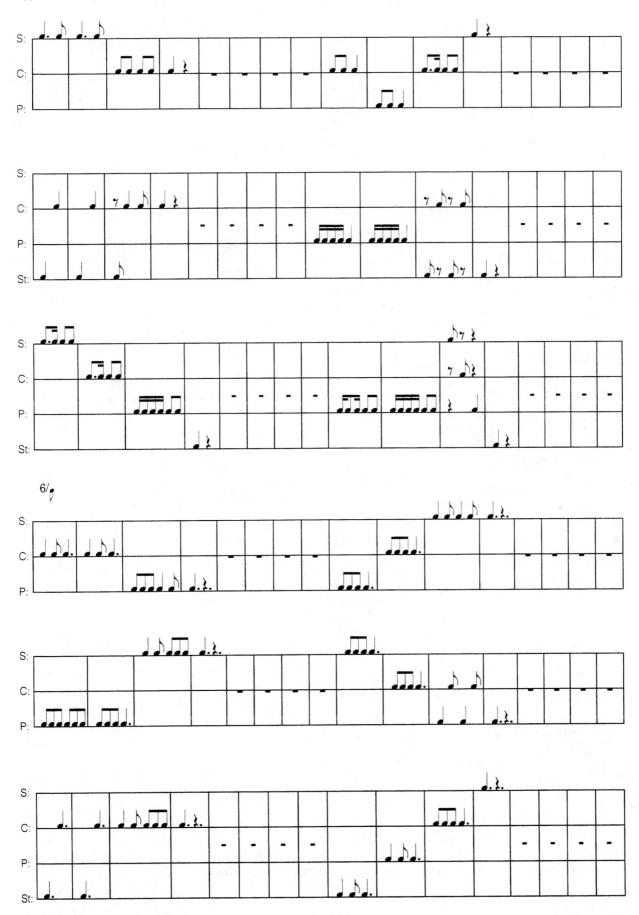

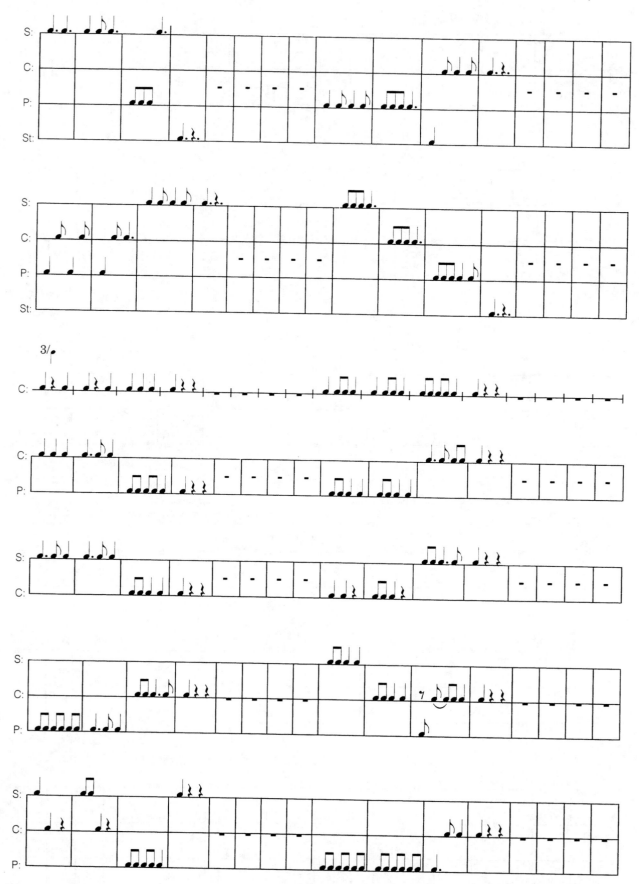

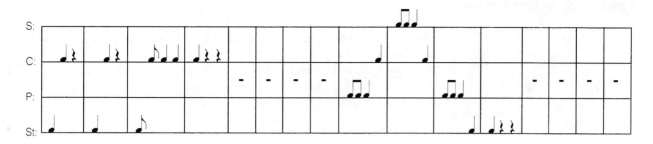

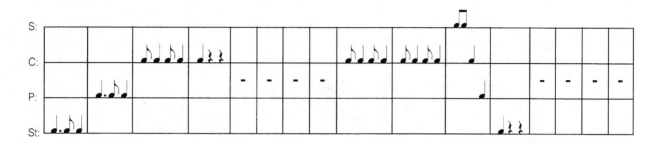

IMITATION FROM BODY PERCUSSION TO UNPITCHED PERCUSSION AND BARRED INSTRUMENTS

Unpitched percussion and barred instruments can be correlated, in timbre, with body percussion.

	Unpitched	*Barred*
Finger snaps	Metals[1]	Soprano & Alto Glockenspiels
Clapping	Woods	Soprano Xylophone Soprano Metallophone
Patting knees	Membranes	Alto Xylophone Alto Metallophone
Stamping	Big Percussion	Bass Xylophone Bass Metallophone

ACTIVITIES

Divide the class into four groups and give each person in the group an instrument in the metal, wood, membrane, or big percussion family. Present rhythmic phrases using body percussion, which are echoed, in groups, by the students. For example, if you presented a pattern using clapping and stamping, it would be echo-played by those with woods and big percussion. See the following example.

TEACHER:

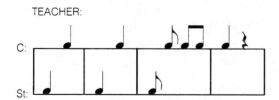

CLASS:

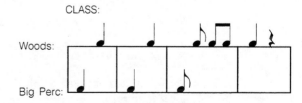

Do the preceding exercise, but use the four groups of barred instruments, in C pentatonic (F's and B's removed).

Try any of the preceding exercises, asking students to close their eyes.

[1]See the Appendix for a complete listing of instruments in families.

MINI-CANON, OR FREE CANON

The mini-canon, or free canon, is an outgrowth and a variation of imitation using body percussion. It demands of the student immediate concentration in order to perform rhythmic patterns correctly. In this exercise, the teacher is always four beats ahead of the student, but now, instead of listening for the student's response, the teacher is presenting a new rhythmic pattern. See the following example.

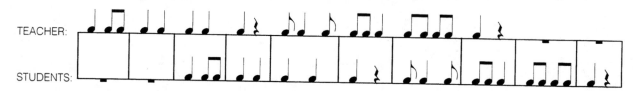

Here are some suggestions for success:

1. Structure the canon over 4 beats in 2/₄ meter.
2. Balance difficult patterns with easy patterns.
3. Vary the levels of body percussion for each pattern.
4. Present each pattern on one level of body percussion only.
5. Be prepared to repeat a difficult pattern.

Additional activities may include the following:

The canons may be done in three or four parts: The teacher presents pattern 1 to group 1; group 1 presents pattern 1 to group 2; and so on.

Students may lead the canon exercise.

OSTINATO WITH SPEECH

The ostinato is a rhythmic, a melodic, or a harmonic structure that is repeated at least once. The word is derived from Latin, *obstinatus*, meaning "stubborn." For children, there are many advantages to using the ostinato as a teaching tool, perhaps the most important being that the entire class is involved from the first moment in making music happen without the necessity for extensive musical knowledge. Some other advantages are that the ostinato

1. Develops a feeling for form
2. Develops memory training
3. Helps strengthen coordination skills
4. Creates an environment in which the player is performing while listening to others
5. Provides a background for improvisation

An ostinato should be more than one measure long to create a musical foundation that allows time for tension and relaxation.

A rhythmic ostinato can be *verbal, vocal,* or *instrumental.*
A melodic ostinato can be *vocal* or *instrumental.*
A harmonic ostinato can be *vocal* or *instrumental.*

Examples given are representative, not comprehensive.

Verbal Ostinato with Poem

ACTIVITIES

I EAT MY PEAS WITH HONEY

I eat my peas with hon-ey, I've done it all my life. It

makes the peas taste fun-ny, But it keeps them on the knife.

OSTINATO

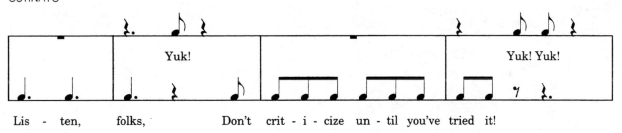

Lis-ten, folks, Yuk! Don't crit-i-cize un-til you've tried it! Yuk! Yuk!

Encourage "interesting" vocal inflection for the poem and the ostinato. Use the ostinato for an introduction and a coda.

I HAD A LITTLE CHICKEN

I had a lit-tle chick-en. She would-n't lay an egg. I poured hot choc'-late up and

down her leg. ___ The lit-tle chick-en wig-gled and the lit-tle chick-en begged. The

lit-tle chick-en laid a hard-boiled egg!

OSTINATO 1

Hard-boiled egg, _ That's what she laid!

OSTINATO 2

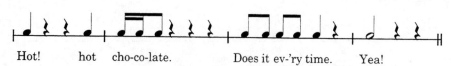

Hot!　hot　cho-co-late.　Does it ev-'ry time.　Yea!

Have the children speak ostinato 1 several times as an introduction, then add the poem. Have them speak ostinato 2 several times, then add the poem. Have them combine the two ostinati and add the poem.

Body Percussion Ostinato with Poem

ACTIVITIES

JELLY BELLY

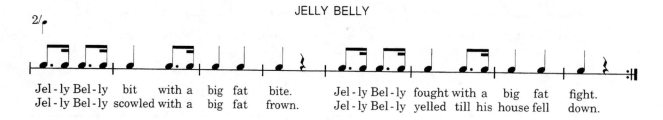

Jel-ly Bel-ly　bit　with a　big fat　bite.　Jel-ly Bel-ly　fought with a　big　fat　fight.
Jel-ly Bel-ly scowled with a　big fat　frown.　Jel-ly Bel-ly　yelled　till his　house fell　down.

OSTINATO

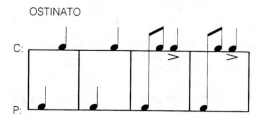

"Jelly Belly" by Dennis Lee from *Jelly Belly* by Dennis Lee, published by Macmillan of Canada © 1983, Dennis Lee.

Ask the children to vary the vocal inflection from verse 1 to verse 2, paying particular attention to the words "Jelly Belly."

Unpitched Percussion Ostinato with Poem

ACTIVITIES

JUST THREE

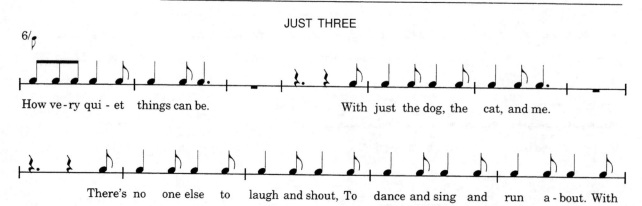

How ve-ry qui - et　things can be.　　With　just　the dog, the　cat, and me.

There's　no　one else　to　laugh and shout, To　dance and sing　and　run　a - bout. With

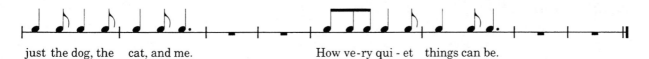

just the dog, the   cat, and me.   How ve-ry qui - et   things can be.

OSTINATO

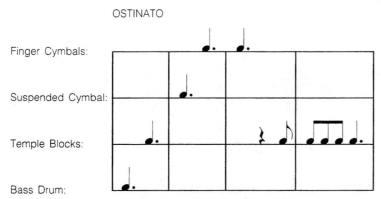

Finger Cymbals:

Suspended Cymbal:

Temple Blocks:

Bass Drum:

"Just Three," from *All on a Summer's Day*. Reprinted by permission of William Wise.
Copyright 1971.

Have the children learn the ostinato by performing it on four levels of body percussion (stamp, knee pats, clap, snap). Then transfer the ostinato to unpitched percussion instruments. Consider transferring words of the poem to hand drums.

Barred Instrumental Ostinati with Speech

ACTIVITIES

Text: Sea gull, sea gull, sit on the sand.
            It's never good weather when you're on the land.

OSTINATI

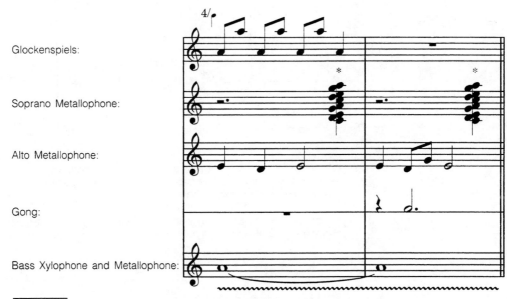

Glockenspiels:

Soprano Metallophone:

Alto Metallophone:

Gong:

Bass Xylophone and Metallophone:

*Play any two notes in A minor pentatonic (F's and B's removed).

Layer the ostinati, one-by-one. Use a soloist to speak the proverb freely. Use the ostinati as an interlude. Ask the entire class to speak the proverb over the sound carpet of the combined ostinati.

OSTINATO WITH SONG

Body Percussion Ostinato with a Song

ACTIVITIES

WE WISH YOU A MERRY DAY

Konnie Saliba

We wish you, wish you, wish you, a mer-ry mer-ry day. We

hope, we hope, we hope, ev-'ry - thing goes your way. With a hey non-ny no and a

hey no non-ny no, We wish you, wish you, wish you, a mer-ry, mer-ry day.

OSTINATO

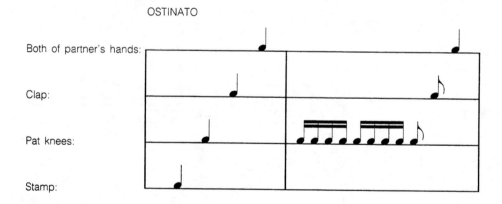

After the children have learned the song, teach the ostinato. Divide the class into partners and allow each set of partners time to practice the pattern at their own tempo before attempting to perform the ostinato with the melody.

Add an interlude consisting of measure 1 of the ostinato repeated four times. Ask each participant to take a walking step on beat 1, and after four patterns be facing a new partner.

SUPERIMPOSED OSTINATI

Verbal

ACTIVITIES
_____

Teach each ostinato to everyone. Use the ostinati as a game: Hold up one finger for ostinato 1, two fingers for ostinato 2, and three fingers for ostinato 3. Ask the class to speak the appropriate ostinato. When everyone knows all three ostinati, divide the class into three sections. Again, indicating with upheld fingers, play the rhythmic game of speaking one ostinato, or two together, or sometimes all three.

Body Percussion

ACTIVITIES
_____

OSTINATO 3

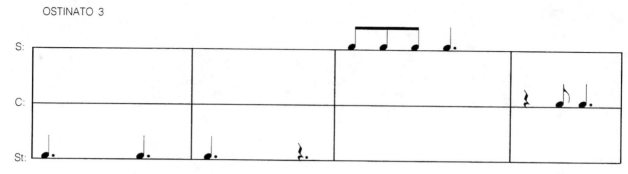

Teach each ostinato to everyone. Play the same game described for verbal superimposed ostinati.

Unpitched Percussion

ACTIVITIES

Teach everyone each ostinato from visual notation, using clapping. Transfer each ostinato to suggested instruments. Layer each ostinato, beginning with 1. Play each new ostinato twice before adding another.

WHEN THE TRAIN COMES ALONG

Spiritual

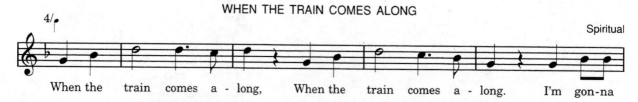

When the train comes a - long, When the train comes a - long. I'm gon-na

meet   you   at   the   sta - tion,   When   the   train   comes   a - long.

OSTINATI

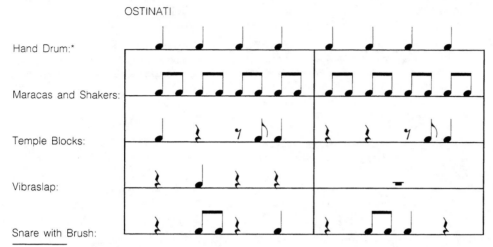

Hand Drum:*

Maracas and Shakers:

Temple Blocks:

Vibraslap:

Snare with Brush:

*With fingernails, make a circular "swish" on the skin of the drum, in a quarter-note pulse.

Layer each ostinato and then add the melody. Use the ostinati as an interlude (with an occasional train whistle). For a coda, eliminate one ostinato at a time.

Barred Instruments

ACTIVITIES

6/ *Lento*

Glockenspiels

Soprano Xylophone, Soprano Metallophone

Alto Xylophone, Alto Metallophone

Bass Xylophone, Bass Metallophone

Teach everyone each ostinato from visual notation by singing. Prepare for transferring patterns to barred instruments by doing such exercises as patting each pattern on the knees, playing patterns "in the air," and playing each pattern on instruments using fingernails.

Layer each ostinato, beginning with the bass instruments. Play each new ostinato twice before adding another.

READING GAMES

Notating Names

Create an A Section and a B Section, using names of children in a class.

ACTIVITIES

Ask individual children in the class to clap their names. Together, notate some names on the chalk-board. Arrange four first and last names into an A Section and four into a B Section. Consider rhythmic contrast for the two sections. Transfer each section to unpitched percussion instruments and create a form (AB; ABA; ABABA).

Arranging Motives

Create a rhythm piece from motives.

ACTIVITIES

Put the four motives on separate visuals, making each visual a different color. Clap a motive and ask the class which one it was; ask the class to clap it. Arrange the motives into a structure that seems correct. Clap the rhythm and then transfer the rhythm to hand drums. Create a speech B Section by making a word chain. Topic choices might be states, rivers, cars, fruits, presidents, and so on.

Changing a Rhythm by the Addition of Dotted Notes

ACTIVITIES

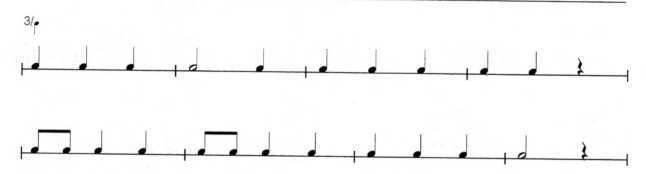

Write a rhythm such as the preceding one on the chalkboard. Ask the class to speak the rhythm in *tas, tees,* and *toes;* clap the rhythm. Ask someone in the class to suggest a place where a quarter note might be changed to a dotted quarter followed by an eighth. Clap the newly changed line and decide if it is a good addition; if not, put the dotted note somewhere else. Continue until the rhythm is as the class likes it. Transfer the rhythm to metal instruments. Add an ostinato.

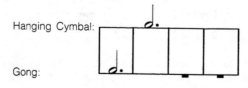

QUESTION-ANSWER IMPROVISATION

From imitation comes improvisation. After children have had many experiences with imitation—with body percussion, unpitched percussion instruments, barred instruments, in movement—they are ready for learning the techniques of question-answer improvisation. Be aware of the following before beginning with classes:

1. The question and the answer should be the same length.
2. There should be elements in the answer phrase that are also in the question phrase.
3. The answer should have a "final point" (that is, it should end on the downbeat of the last measure).
4. The question should not have a "final point."

The following sections give you suggestions for ways to begin.

Using "International" Language

Ask each child in the class to hold up four fingers on one hand, and with the other point to one finger after the other while counting 1-2-3-4-5-6-7-8. This structure will help children to maintain the phrase length when they begin their answering phrases. (Do expect mistakes; it is part of the learning process.) Then give the class a question phrase in "international" language[2] and have the class, collectively, provide the answer. For example:

vo zee   dah dee, vo   zee dah, vo   zee dah do ee?

vo zee dah, vo zee dah loo a be say gnor!

For this to be successful, you must use a wide variety of vocal sounds, with great dynamic and range differences.

Rather than ask for collective answers, ask answers of individual children.

See if there are some children who can provide a question phrase to the class.

Using Body Percussion

Clap a phrase of rhythm in 2/♩ meter for the class. Ask them to give you a collective answer, using the *first* part of the phrase they hear for the *first* part of their answering phrase, and to change the ending. For example:

[2]Another term for international language is *nonsense language,* consisting of a series of consonant and vowel sounds that have no literal meaning.

Provide at least a dozen question phrases for a class, to allow them opportunity to use half of what they hear as an answering phrase.

Ask the class to use the *last* part of the phrase they hear for the *first* part of their answering phrase, again changing the ending. For example:

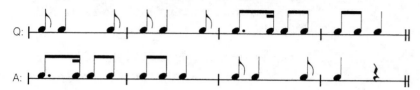

Eventually, ask the children to incorporate *any* motive they hear into their answering phrase. For example:

Ask the children to provide an answer to the phrase they hear, but to use a different level of body percussion.

Tell the children they may use any *two* levels of body percussion for the answering phrase.

Using Unpitched Percussion Instruments

Divide the class into three groups. One group has metal instruments, one has wood instruments, and the third has membrane instruments. If you give a question phrase on a wood instrument, only the woods answer; a metal, only metals; a drum, only membranes.

For variation, ask a child to provide a question phrase for the class.

Using Barred Instruments

For first experiences in improvisation, use a pentatonic scale, such as C (F's and B's removed). At first, don't specify that the final note of the answer be tonic; that can occur later. Also, for musical melodies, ask the children to always begin answers by "walking upward" from where they begin, or "walking downward" or "up and down" or "down and up." (This provides stepwise melodies.) A good instrument for you to use is a glockenspiel.

At first, allow all children playing instruments to provide "collective" answers. Later, specify that "glockenspiels give the answer."

If there are not enough barred instruments, include unpitched percussion, from the wood and metal families of instruments.

Later, allow the children to experience question-answer in modes, such as Dorian.

Using Movement

At the piano, improvise four measures of 2/♩, and ask the children to move appropriately, freezing into statues at the end of the phrase. After the phrase length is secure, divide the class into partners. One partner moves and makes a statue with improvisation in the high register of the piano; the other does the same with the low register. Each statue is made with the partner.

Change the meter to 6/♪.

Question-Answer as the B Section

BE MY PARTNER

Konnie Saliba

Be my part-ner and im-pro-vise with me. Be my part-ner, Doo-ble-de-do be dee.

Have the children form a circle and sing "Be My Partner," adding a simple step-snap movement. In the center of the circle are two instruments, such as a conga and temple blocks. After singing A, the child playing temple blocks gives a rhythmic question to the child at the conga, who provides the answer. Then during the repeat of A, the child who played the temple blocks gives the mallets to the child who played the conga. The temple block player returns to the circle but also selects someone to play the conga for the next B Section. This game can be continued for a long time.

Rondo

The rondo form is still another way to encourage improvisation. The rondo is particularly suitable for small-group improvisation or for improvisation by families of instruments.

Rondo for Body Percussion

Teach the A Section through imitation. Teach everyone the ostinato. Divide the class into partners. Partner A does the rhythm and partner B the ostinato. Select some children who would like to provide the B, C, D sections, and so on, using body percussion. Encourage levels other than clapping, since the A Section uses clapping.

Rondo for Unpitched Percussion Instruments

For B, C, and D sections, and so on, select small families of contrasting instruments, such as a conga, a guiro, and a cow bell; a hand drum, claves, and a cabaza.

Rondo for Barred Instruments

Soprano Xylophone

OSTINATI

Alto Xylophone

Alto Metallophone

Bass Xylophone

Place all barred instruments into F pentatonic (B's and E's removed). The B, C, and D sections can be improvised by families of glockenspiels, xylophones, and metallophones, or by soloists who volunteer.

Rondo for Singing and Unpitched Percussion Instruments

ACTIVITIES

_____

ONE LITTLE MONKEY

Konnie Saliba

One lit-tle, two lit-tle, three lit-tle mon-kies. Four lit-tle, five lit-tle, six lit-tle mon-kies.

Sev'n lit-tle, eight lit-tle, nine lit-tle mon-kies. Ten lit-tle mon-kies im-pro-vise.

Select ten soloists, who will play ten different unpitched percussion instruments. Place them in a line, facing the class. The first instrument is "monkey 1," the last "monkey 10." The A Section is the song. This is followed by an improvisation (the length of the song) by 1. A is repeated and the improvisation occurs by 1 and 2. A is repeated and improvisation is done by 1, 2, and 3, and so on until all are improvising.

Melody

WAYS TO TEACH MELODY

1. *Echo singing:* Sing melodic phrases for the class in solfeggio with Curwen hand signs;[3] ask them to echo-sing, using their hand signs.

2. *Recognition of motives of a melody:* Make visualizations of the different parts of a melody and place in random order on a board. Play or sing the entire melody and ask the class to arrange it correctly. For example:

Motives:

(a)

(b)

(c)

Melody:

CAPTAIN, GO SIDETRACK YOUR TRAIN

Folk Song

Cap-tain, go side-track your train.   Cap-tain, go side-track your train.   Num-ber three in

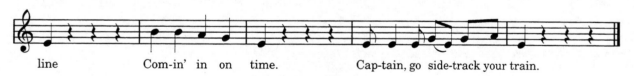

line   Com-in' in on time.   Cap-tain, go side-track your train.

3. *Recognizing, singing, and playing motives:*

[3]For Curwen hand signs, see the Appendix.

Metallophones

Basses

Number the phrases 1–4. Sing a phrase for the class on a neutral syllable. While they are internalizing the sound, ask the class to show, with fingers in the air, whether you sang phrase 1, 2, 3, or 4. Then have them sing the phrase on a neutral syllable and with letter names; have them play the phrase on instruments. Repeat the process enough times that everyone has had opportunity to play each motive several times. When the children have learned all four motives, divide the class into four sections. Ask those playing basses to play their pattern twice and continue playing while all metallophones are added, all xylophones, all glockenspiels.

4. *Dictation:* Tell the class the starting note. Then sing a motive on a neutral syllable. For example:

Have the class echo-sing on a neutral syllable and then with letter names. Have them play the motive on instruments. Hint: Begin with stepwise motives, because skips are difficult.

5. *Hand staff:*

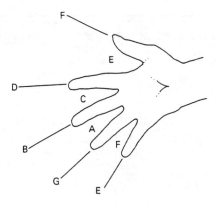

Hold one hand in front of the body, fingers spread; with the other hand, point and simultaneously sing a pattern. Ask the class to model by echo singing and using their hand staves. (To show a sharp, use two fingers; to show a flat, bend the index finger.)

6. *Soprano recorder:* Introduce playing the soprano recorder to improve reading skills.

7. *Inner hearing:* Clap the rhythm of a familiar melody—for example, "London Bridge"—and see if the class can recognize the melody from the rhythm. Ask children in the class to contribute.

PENTATONIC SCALES

A pentatonic scale is, by definition, five different notes within the distance of an octave. The pentatonic used in Orff-Schulwerk is without half steps, which makes it especially suitable for improvisation. By removing bars on Orff instruments, you can easily form the following pentatonic scales.

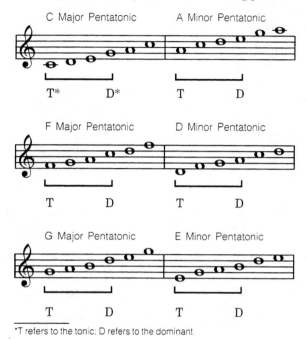

*T refers to the tonic; D refers to the dominant.

The following are some of the advantages of using pentatonic scales.

1. All tones may sound sound together, because without the half steps, there is no tension.
2. Without half steps, a single-harmony accompaniment (the bordun) may be used.
3. The pentatonic has an open, stressfree feeling, which is calming for the child.
4. Using pentatonic melodies, with their appropriate accompaniments, can stimulate creativity in improvisation activities and in the creation of new melodies.

C Major Pentatonic

ACTIVITIES

DON'T LET THE WIND

St. Helena's Island

Don't let the wind, Don't let the wind, Don't let the wind blow here no more. Oh, _____

don't let the wind, Don't let the wind blow here no more.

ACCOMPANIMENT
Soprano and Alto Glockenspiels

Soprano and Alto Metallophones

Bass Xylophone and Metallophone

*Play any two notes in C pentatonic.

Teach the melody by showing a visual of measure 1 and then playing the melody for the class on a recorder, asking them to tell how many times they hear the motive.

After the children have learned the song and have added instrument parts, create a B Section, which is a storm. The following preparation can be done:

Wind	=		=	Glissandos on xylophones
Rain	=		=	Glockenspiels, lightly
Clouds	=		=	Any two notes, metallophones
Thunder	=		=	Timpani and cymbal

Make a visual at the board and ask a child to use a mallet and slowly create the storm by moving the mallet through the visual, from left to right.

A Minor Pentatonic

ACTIVITIES

HOP-A-DOODLE

American Folk Song

Down in the mead-ow, Hop-a-doo-dle, Hop-a-doo-dle. Down in the barn-yard,

Hop-a-doo-dle doo. Down in the mead-ow the colt be-gan to prance. The cow be-gan to

whis-tle, and the pig be-gan to dance.

BORDUN: Bass Xylophone

Teach one or more of the following body percussion patterns, and add them as an introduction and a coda.

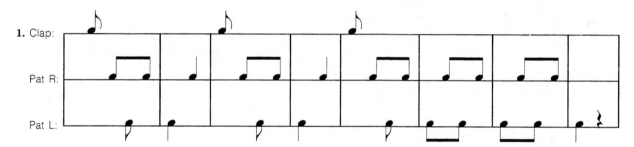

1. Clap:

Pat R:

Pat L:

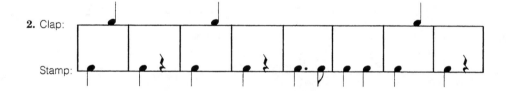

2. Clap:

Stamp:

3. Clap:

F Major Pentatonic

ACTIVITIES

HOLD MY MULE

American Folk Song

Hold my mule while I dance, Jo-sie, Hold my mule while I dance, Jo-sie, Oh, Miss Su-san Brown.

BORDUN
Alto Metallophone

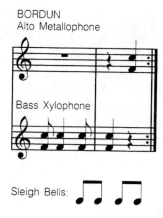

Bass Xylophone

Sleigh Bells:

Create a B Section, using alto and soprano xylophones and four levels of unpitched percussion instruments.

Xylophones:

Vibraslap:

Cow Bell:

Guiro:

Bass Drum:

Create a form based upon the A and B sections.

D Minor Pentatonic

ACTIVITIES

IF I WERE A LIZARD

Konnie Saliba

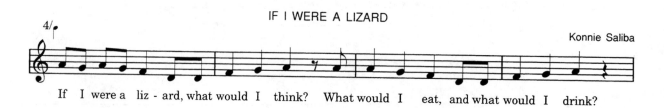

If I were a liz - ard, what would I think? What would I eat, and what would I drink?

Where would I live and how would it be? If I were a liz - ard, would you like me?

ACCOMPANIMENT
Bass Xylophone

Log Drum:

Make two melodic visuals of phrases from the melody.

1.   **2.**

As the class listens to the melody in its entirety, ask them to observe whether they hear phrase 1 or phrase 2. On the second hearing, ask them to raise one or two fingers to indicate which phrase they are hearing.

Create a B Section.

On the chalkboard, write the following sequence of incomplete sentences. Have the class complete the sentences.

I'd think like a lizard,
I'd eat _____
I'd drink _____
And live _____
If I were a lizard
I'm sure you can see.
You would most likely
Really like me!

Consider adding unpitched percussion instruments to the B Section.

For an added verse, replace the word "lizard" with another name.

G Major Pentatonic

ACTIVITIES

OLD GREY GOOSE

Southern Folk Song

Look-a-right here and   look-a-right there.   Look 'way o - ver yon-der.   Don't you see the

old grey goose a - smil-in' at the gan-der.   A - smil-in',   a - smil-in',   a - smil-in' at the gander.

ACCOMPANIMENT
Alto Metallophone

Bass Xylophone

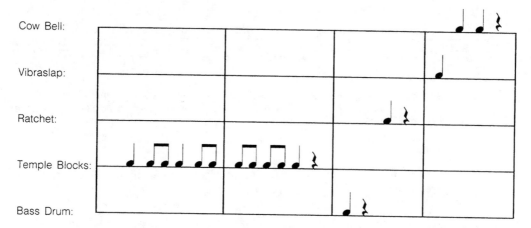

Discuss how a goose walks and how it holds its head. Let the children create movement for the melody. Have them sing the melody with movement; have them internalize the words over the accompaniment so that there are accompaniment and movement only.

E Minor Pentatonic

ACTIVITIES

SUNSET

Dakota Indian

When the   moon _ is   in   the   sky.   Fa-ther sun sleeps in the west.   And his peo-ple go to _   rest.
To   the   sun _ we say good-bye.

Alto Xylophone,
Alto Metallophone +

Bass Xylophone,
Bass Metallophone +

+ Tremolo softly throughout entire melody on two notes in E minor pentatonic,
changing notes occasionally.

Create a B Section that uses the rhythm of the words as follows:

When the <u>moon</u> is in the sky.
To the <u>sun</u> we say goodbye.
Father sun <u>sleeps</u> in the <u>west</u>.
And his <u>people</u> go to <u>rest</u>.

Ask the class to internalize the words to create the B Section and transfer the underlined words to the following instruments:

moon	=	Gong
sun	=	Hanging cymbal
sleeps	=	Finger cymbals
west and *rest*	=	Bell tree
people	=	Triangle

HEXATONIC MELODY
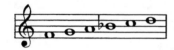

ACTIVITIES

SING HEY

Konnie Saliba

Sing   hey, sing hey, sing hey, sing hey, sing hey for Christ-mas day.   Sing   for Christ-mas   day.

Win-ter, win-ter, win-ter, win-ter, win-ter snows.   We are hap-py, hap-py, hap-py friend-ship grows.

ACCOMPANIMENT
Alto Xylophone

Bass Xylophone, Bass Metallophone

Sleigh Bells:

Dance

A: In a circle formation, the children hold their hands high and move forward counterclockwise.

B: The circle moves in to the center and out; the children hold their hands low, raising them as the circle moves in, lowering them as the circle moves out.

THE MAJOR SCALE

ACTIVITIES

BLACK-EYED-SUSIE

Southern Folk Song

All I want in this cre - a - tion, Pret-ty lit-tle wife on a big plan-ta-tion.

Hey, _ lit-tle black-eyed Su-sie, Hey, _ lit-tle black-eyed Su-sie, Hey. _____

ACCOMPANIMENT
Soprano Xylophone

Alto Metallophone

Bass Xylophone

*At cadence.

Verse 2. All I want to make me happy,
Two little boys to call me Pappy.

Verse 3. Love my wife and love my baby,
Love my biscuits sopped in gravey.

Add a body percussion game, such as the following one, to be done while singing. Divide the class into partners, spaced freely throughout the room.

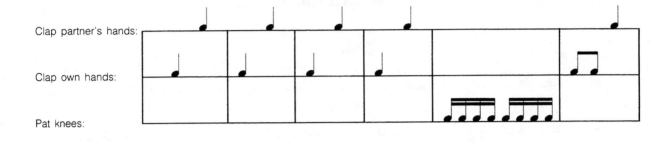

Movement

The movement ideas contained in this chapter are examples of what can be done with beginners as well as with those with more experience. The teacher with movement experience will be able to select exercises and adapt and modify them to fit the needs of specific groups of children. The teacher who is not so secure in movement should be able to incorporate the simple exercises into the teaching technique.

LOCOMOTOR ACTIVITIES WITH BODY PERCUSSION

ACTIVITIES

Review walking (♩ ♩), running (♫ ♫), and skipping (♪♩ ♪♩). Divide the class into three groups and ask each group to move in the space only when hearing their assigned rhythm, and to bounce in place when others are moving.

Variation: Rather than using an instrument for the rhythmic values, speak the word "walk," "run," or "skip."

Add shapes to a walking exercise. Consider some of the following: walking in curved lines, in straight lines, in a figure eight, in own circle.

Have the children walk and echo-clap rhythmic patterns in different meters. For example:

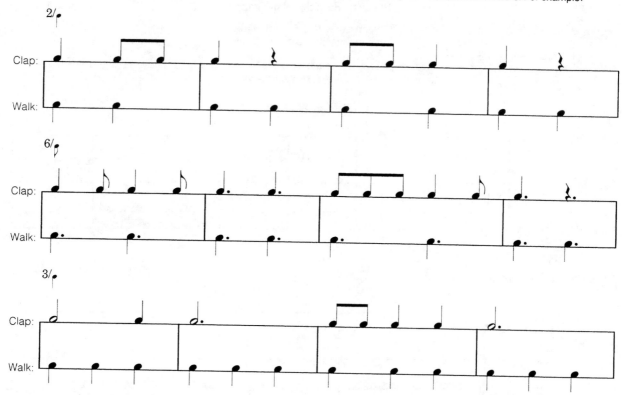

Have the children walk and echo patterns you give on hand-held unpitched percussion instruments.

Have the children create movement patterns in phrases, using the stamp and the clap. For example:

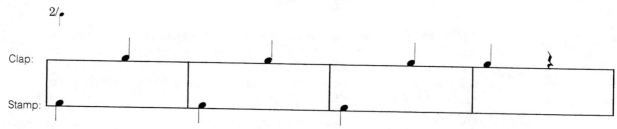

Using the same pattern or a similar one, choose a formation, such as a line, and have the children move forward for a phrase and backward for a phrase.

Place the class in partner formation. Have the children move away from their partners for a phrase, and toward their partners for a phrase.

Have the children move around their partners.

Add speech to a movement body percussion pattern. (The movement pattern could be forward, backward, into the center of a circle, out, and so on.) For example:

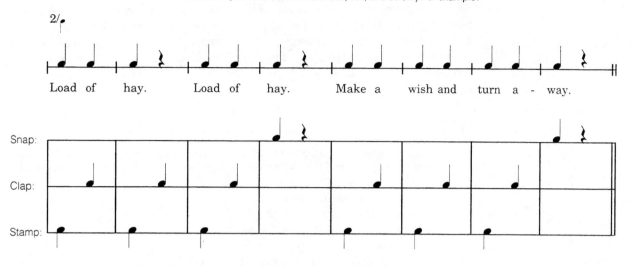

Have the children combine walking and skipping patterns. For example:

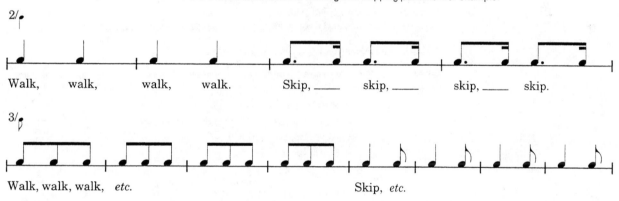

Let the children create body percussion patterns using 3/♩ and 2/♩. For example:

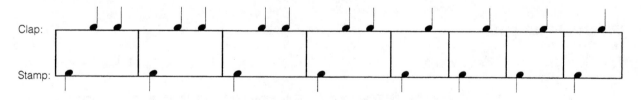

Have the children create a pattern for the feet and move while singing a melody. For example:

METER

By definition, meter is the division of time into measures by means of regularly recurring accents, the first of which is the strongest accent. Meter is measure and has no rhythm. The following activities represent some ways to allow children to experience meter and to feel the change from one meter to another. It is the teacher's responsibility to repeat each meter a number of times to assure success.

ACTIVITIES

Ask the class to walk continuously at a moderate tempo and consider each step a beat. Create a feeling of 4/♩ by emphasizing beat 1 with movement of the arms and entire body. Add counting aloud while moving: *one,* two, three, four.

> Change to 3/♩: *one,* two, three
> Change to 2/♩: *one,* two
> Change to 5/♩: *one,* two, three, four, five
> Change to 6/♩: *one,* two, three, four, five, six
> Change to 7/♩: *one,* two, three, four, five, six, seven

Variations: Play the accent of the measure on an unpitched percussion instrument. Give each child a tennis ball and ask him or her to bounce the ball on the accent. Create games by combining walking with bouncing the ball or by tossing the ball to a partner on the accent.

Create a group meter game using 2/♩, 3/♩, 4/♩, and 6/♪.

Game 1: Play the timpani with an accent to show the meter. Ask the class to respond in the following ways:

> 2/♩ ♩♩   = Stand in place and nod head.
> 3/♩ ♩♩♩   = Each child invents his or her own movement.
> 4/♩ ♩♩♩♩   = Walk in space, clap on accent.
> 6/♪ ♩♪♩♩   = Skip in space.

Game 2:

> 2/♩ ♩♩   = Walk with a partner.
> 3/♩ ♩♩♩   = Walk in threes.
> 4/♩ ♩♩♩♩   = Walk in fours.
> 6/♪ ♩♪♩♩   = Skip or gallop alone.

IRREGULAR MEASURE

ACTIVITIES

Create irregular measures by accenting another beat within the measure. For example, in a measure of eight:

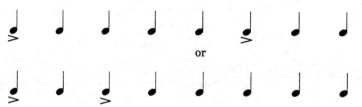

Accents may be shown by moving and counting aloud or by clapping. Each person may also show the accent by playing it on an unpitched percussion instrument.

SPEECH AND MOVEMENT IN THE METERS OF 3/♪, 2/♪, AND 5/♪

ACTIVITIES

Poem in 3/♪

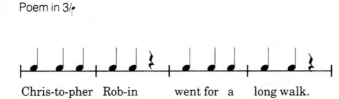

Chris-to-pher Rob-in   went for a   long walk.

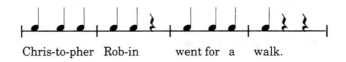

Chris-to-pher Rob-in   went for a   walk.

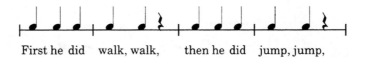

First he did   walk, walk,   then he did   jump, jump,

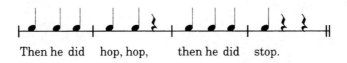

Then he did   hop, hop,   then he did   stop.

Poem in 2/♪

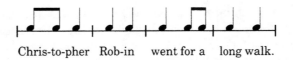

Chris-to-pher Rob-in   went for a   long walk.

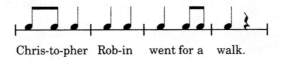

Chris-to-pher Rob-in   went for a   walk.

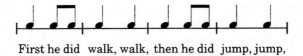

First he did walk, walk, then he did jump, jump,

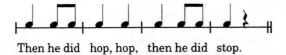

Then he did   hop, hop,   then he did   stop.

Poem in 5/₄

Chris-to-pher Rob-in   went for a long walk.

Chris-to-pher Rob-in   went for a walk.

First he did walk, walk, then he did jump, jump,

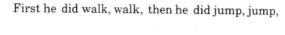

Then he did hop, hop,   then he did stop.

Ask the class to speak each poem, showing a vocal accent on the strong beat. Ask them to speak and move; to speak, move, and clap on the accent. Ask them to internalize the words and move and clap on the accent.

Variation: Transfer accents to unpitched percussion instruments. Perform the locomotor movements suggested in the words.

IMPROVISATION

Movement improvisation, also referred to in previous chapters as creative movement, should begin early and be nurtured and encouraged throughout a child's development. There are some children, particularly young ones, who move freely, without inhibition. They are likely to remain this way into their developing childhood. But there are others who lack confidence and feel inhibited in spontaneous movement. It is a task of the sensitive teacher to distinguish between the child who feels comfortable in spontaneous movement and the one who does not. Also, it should not be assumed that saying to a student, "Move any way you feel like," will result in beauty or form. On the contrary, such statements will usually produce less than musical results and various levels of insecurity for many of the participants. It is a task of the teacher to guide all children and, when seeing an idea, to make positive comments toward the achievement of such things as balance and form. Ideas presented here are to help provide a focus that may encourage children to want to contribute.

ACTIVITIES

Individual Improvisation within the Group

Teach the class to sing, or ask them to listen to, an 8-measure melody and, together, create a floor pattern for the melody, which is the A Section. Ask each child to move appropriately in space when he or she hears you play an improvised B Section, returning to the floor pattern for a repeat of A.

Variations: Several individuals may improvise B-Section movement while the class adds a stamp-clap accompaniment. A rondo can be created by choosing small groups to provide the contrasting sections (B, C, D, and so on).

(As the teacher, be sensitive to the fact that children of this age should be allowed to improvise in ways suitable to their personalities. There should be a balance between flowing patterns and vigorous rhythms.)

Partner Improvisation

Divide the class into partners. One partner in each set is A; the other is B. As you improvise a melody at the piano—for example, in the high register—the A children improvise movement for their partners. This is immediately followed by improvised movement by B, perhaps in relation to the low register of the piano. (Two timbres of unpitched percussion may be used.) Encourage such ideas as

  a. Relating in movement with the partner regarding such things as level, intensity, and floor pattern
  b. Making a statue with the partner at the end of each phrase
  c. Accompanying the improvisation with hand-held unpitched percussion instruments or with mouth sounds
  d. Suggesting verbal ideas to help focus the improvisation, such as words like "flowing," "angry," "frightened," "surprised," "happy"

Divide the class into partners. One child is the sculptor and one the person to be sculptured. The sculptor is to form the partner's body into a "living" piece of sculpture, being aware of level, shape, and structure, but also being kind to think about the partner's comfort. When the sculptors are finished, they sit and appraise the sculpture around them before switching roles.

Small-Group Improvisation

Divide the class into groups of three or four. Ask each group to decide upon a means of locomotion and a sound to accompany it. Allow each group time to experiment before sharing with other participants.

Divide the class into groups of four to six. Ask each group to create a machine in which each participant is a functioning part. Suggest that the machine use nonlocomotor movements and perhaps locomotor, and that the machine be accompanied by selected unpitched percussion instrument sounds.

Divide the class into groups of five or more and ask each group to form a circle. Select a leader for each circle. Allow each circle time to discover, without speaking, how many ways the leader can indicate that the circle, as a whole, move. Ideas could include moving inward, outward, forward, backward, sinking, rising, fast, slow, and so on.

Variation: Improvise without a leader.

Divide the class into groups of three or more. Each group forms a line with the head member leading movement, which is imitated by those behind. Change leaders.

CANONS

Rhythm for Body Percussion, with a Floor Pattern

Have the children learn the rhythm by rote and practice until it is correct. Have them learn the pattern for the feet before they combine it with the rhythm. Allow time for the class to move and clap in their own space before adding the turn. Divide the class into four groups and place a group in each corner of the room. Each group moves diagonally toward the center of the room, turning at the last beat of measure 4 to return to its original place. Perform in four-part canon. Improvised unpitched percussion accompaniment may be added, with strong emphasis on the quarter-note pulse.

Locomotor Movement Canon, Accompanied by Unpitched Percussion

In a moderate 4/♩ tempo, teach the following sequence:

Phrase 1: With one foot, "paw" the ground for 8 beats.
Phrase 2: Prance forward, with small high steps, for 8 beats.
Phrase 3: With one hand, imitate cracking a whip, beginning low and getting higher, in 4 half-note beats.
Phrase 4: Each person gallops in his or her individual circle for 6 beats, hitting hands to the floor on beat 7.

ACTIVITIES

Teach each phrase to the entire class and have them practice until all four are memorized and accurate. Add a different unpitched percussion instrument for each phrase as follows:

Phrase 1 = Tambourine
Phrase 2 = Sleigh bells
Phrase 3 = Whip
Phrase 4 = Wood block

Practice the entire sequence in unison with instruments. Divide the class into two groups and have them perform in a two-part canon, the second group entering after 8 beats. Perform in a four-part canon.

Unison Song with Movement in Four-Part Canon

ACTIVITIES

STREETS OF LAREDO

American Folk Song

As   I was a-walk-ing the streets of La-re-do, As   I walked out in La-re-do one day.   I spied a young

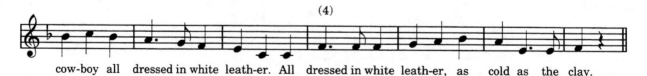

cow-boy all   dressed in white leath-er. All   dressed in white leath-er, as   cold as   the clay.

Be certain the class knows the song thoroughly before adding movement. As a preliminary step, ask all members of the class to face you and sing together. As all sing, perform a movement for the length of the first phrase (for example, swaying in place). During the second phrase of the melody, the class will add the swaying movement, at which time you will perform something new (like walking in your own circle). When this sequence is secure, divide the class into two to four circles, one inside the other. All sing in unison, and the innermost circle, whose leader chooses the movement for each phrase, adds movement. In phrase 2, the movement is done by the next circle; and so on until all circles are moving.

Variation: The melody can be hummed or sung on "oo." The singing can be eliminated for a number of phrases and then sung again.

Melody and Movement in Canon

ACTIVITIES

Melody

TWENTY-FOUR ROBBERS

Konnie Saliba

Last _night, night be-fore. Twen-ty-four rob-bers at my door. I got up, let them in.

Hit them on the head with a roll-ing pin. Du-du - du-du-. . . . .

Movement: Line Formation in Four Groups

1.

Step forward four "jazzy" steps, Backward four "jazzy" steps.

2.

Stoop down, imitate pulling door open. Hit fists together four times.

3.

Wave right hand; make a complete circle to right for eight beats.

4.

Sway. R snap.   Sway. L snap.   Sway. R snap.   Snap   snap.

Teach with the following sequence: melody only; movement only; melody and movement in unison; melody and movement in two-part canon; melody and movement in four-part canon.

Suggestion for the form:

Perform as melody and movement in unison.

Melody and movement in four-part canon, performed twice.

Movement without melody in four-part canon, once.

Using Orff Instruments

Instrumental experiences with upper elementary students can include the following:

1. Harmonic accompaniments: I–V; I–IV–V; I–VII or I–II; I–VI or I–III
2. Syncopated accompaniments
3. Extended forms, such as the rondo
4. Playing melodies
5. Multiple ostinati, for barred instruments and for unpitched percussion instruments
6. Instrumental pieces for specific groups of instruments

I–V ACCOMPANIMENTS

Key of G Major

ACTIVITIES

Make a visual showing the rhythm of measures 1 and 2. Clap the rhythm. Speak the words of the song in rhythm to the class and ask them to indicate how many times they hear the same rhythm.

Key of F Major, with Group Improvisation

ACTIVITIES

TOADS ARE MY BEST FRIENDS

Konnie Saliba

A SECTION

I had a lit - tle toad, and he had a lit-tle pal, And the three of us were friends.
We ne-ver were __ sad, and we al-ways had a grin, And __ that's why we were friends.

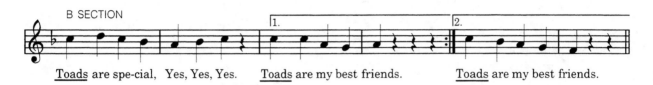

B SECTION

Toads are spe-cial, Yes, Yes, Yes. Toads are my best friends. Toads are my best friends.

ACCOMPANIMENT
Glockenspiels

Alto Metallophone

Bass Xylophone

I   V   I

Ask a child to play the underlined word, "toads," on a ratchet each time it occurs in the B Section.

Create an added section by selecting three instruments to represent the "toads," and ask three children to improvise as a small family. Make the improvisation the length of the A or the B Section. For group improvisation, encourage the children to listen to one another and not play continuously.

Key of G Major, with Multiple Ostinati for Unpitched Percussion Instruments

ACTIVITIES

HALLELU

Trinidad Folk Song

Sing to the mu - sic, Hal - le - lu. __   Sing to the mu - sic, Hal - le - lu. __

Sing to the mu-sic, Hal-le-lu. __

ACCOMPANIMENT

Before adding barred instruments, have the class try singing each part, using letter names. Divide the class and ask one-half to sing the melody, one-half the bass part.

I–IV–V ACCOMPANIMENTS

Key of F Major, with "Special" Words on Unpitched Percussion Instruments

ACTIVITIES

EV'RY ONE BUT ME

New England Folk Song

O the fox and the hare and the bad-ger and the bear and the squirrel in the wal-nut tree. And the

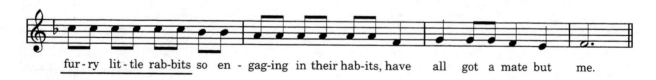

fur - ry lit - tle rab-bits so en - gag-ing in their hab-its, have all got a mate but me.

ACCOMPANIMENT

Verse 2. Oh the <u>lark</u> and the <u>wren</u>, and the <u>cuckoo</u> in the glen,
And the <u>owl</u> in the hollow tree.
And the <u>jaybird</u> and the <u>hawk</u> with a cry and a squawk,
Have all got a nest but me.

Verse 3. Oh, the <u>fish</u> and the <u>frog</u> and the <u>turtle</u> and the <u>dog</u>,
And the <u>worm</u> in the old oak tree.
And the <u>frisky little rat</u>, and the <u>big fat cat,</u>
Have all got a home but me.

Make a visual of all the verses with the underlined words. Have the children sing each verse and, while singing, clap each underlined word, being certain to clap each syllable. Have them internalize each verse and clap only on underlined words. Transfer each underlined word to a different unpitched percussion instrument. Have the children perform each verse, singing with accompaniment; then have only unpitched percussion instruments perform over the accompaniment.

Key of G Major, with Multiple Ostinati for Unpitched Percussion Instruments

ACTIVITIES

COLON MAN

Jamaica

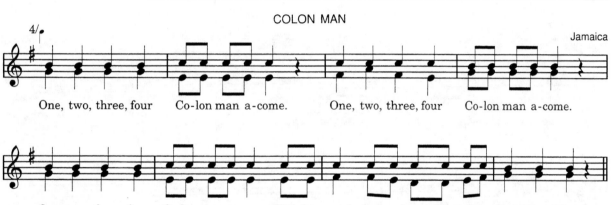

One, two, three, four   Co-lon man a-come.   One, two, three, four   Co-lon man a-come.

One, two, three, four   Co-lon man a-come, With his watch chain a-knock him bel-ly, Pum! Pum! Pum!

ACCOMPANIMENT
Soprano Metallophone

Bass Xylophone, Guitar

I   IV   V   I

Maracas:

Cow Bell:

Claves:

Bongos:

Conga:

Verse 2.   Ask him for the time an' he look up at the sun. (*Repeat twice more.*)
With the brass chain a-knock him belly, Pum! Pum! Pum!

Consider singing a harmony part to the melody (upward stems) and playing the two parts on soprano recorders for added verses.

Add a dance in partner formation, partners spaced freely in the room. Boys can put hands on their back pockets; girls can pretend to hold the ruffles on their skirts.

Step: (Samba)

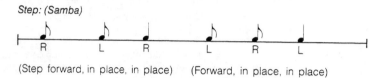

R   L   R   L   R   L

(Step forward, in place, in place)   (Forward, in place, in place)

Variations with the samba step include partners moving around one another or in their own circle.

Key of F Major

ACTIVITIES

A CRAZY SONG

Konnie Saliba

Draw a fun - ny pic - ture,   Write a cra - zy poem.   Sing   a loon - ey goon - ey song and
Do   a hok - ey pok - ey dance,   'cross the kitch-en floor.

whis-tle through your comb.   Put some-thing sil - ly in the world that ain't been there be-fore.

ACCOMPANIMENT
Alto Xylophone

Bass Xylophone, Guitar

Temple Blocks:

Cabaza:

Vibraslap:

Create movement for the melody as follows:

Measures 1–4: Pantomime according to the suggestion of the words.
Measures 5–6: Join hands with a partner, and do the "hokey-pokey."

Measures 7–8: Improvise "something silly."

Let the children sing and move; have them perform the movement with accompaniment but without singing.

I–II ACCOMPANIMENT

Key of C Major

ACTIVITIES

LAUGH AND SING

Konnie Saliba

We can laugh and we can sing. We can do al-most an-y-thing. We

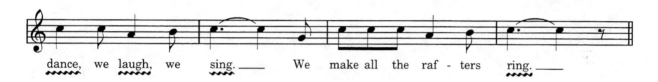

dance, we laugh, we sing.____ We make all the raf-ters ring.____

ACCOMPANIMENT
Glockenspiels

Bass, Alto, Soprano Xylophones

Double Bass Bars

I   II   I

Create an A₁ Section by speaking the words rhythmically over the accompaniment and transferring all underlined words to metal unpitched percussion instruments such as sleigh bells, triangles, and tambourines.

I–VII ACCOMPANIMENT

Key of G Minor

ACTIVITIES

BELIEVE IT OR NOT

Konnie Saliba

On Thurs-day I al-ways say a pray'r That Fri-day will soon be here. And

do   you   know,   to   this   ve - ry   day,   so   far   I've   al - ways   had   my   way.

ACCOMPANIMENT
Glockenspiels (Countermelody)

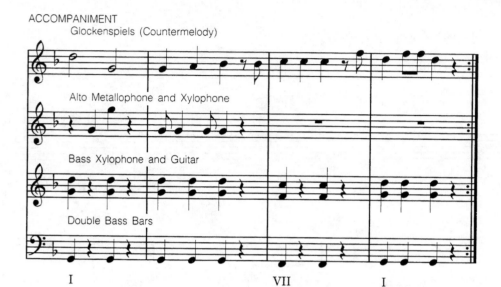

Alto Metallophone and Xylophone

Bass Xylophone and Guitar

Double Bass Bars

I   VII   I

Consider playing the melody on soprano recorders or on a flute.

Add a dance in a line or circle formation.

Dance: The first four measures are a modified grapevine step.[4]

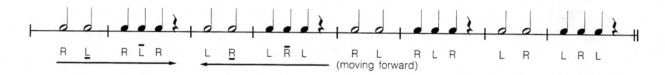

R   L   R L R   L   R   L R L   R L   R L R   L R   L R L
                        (moving forward)

I–VI ACCOMPANIMENT

Key of C Major, with Multiple Ostinati for Unpitched Percussion Instruments

ACTIVITIES

IN A GENTLE STYLE

Konnie Saliba

Soprano and Tenor Recorders

[4]A line under the designated foot means to cross behind; a line on top means to cross over.

ACCOMPANIMENT

Keep the atmosphere of the melody slow and gentle. Create a chain rondo by grouping small families of unpitched percussion instruments and asking the players of the instruments to provide added B, C, D sections, and so on, for the length of the melody, always returning for a repeat of the A Section.

I–III ACCOMPANIMENT

Key of D Minor

ACTIVITIES

BOLIVIAN STYLE

Konnie Saliba

III

A SECTION

B SECTION

Teach the melody with two melodic visuals, one of measure 1, the other of measure 9.

SYNCOPATED ACCOMPANIMENTS

Simple Bordun: F Pentatonic

ACTIVITIES

WIGGLE AND GIGGLE

Konnie Saliba

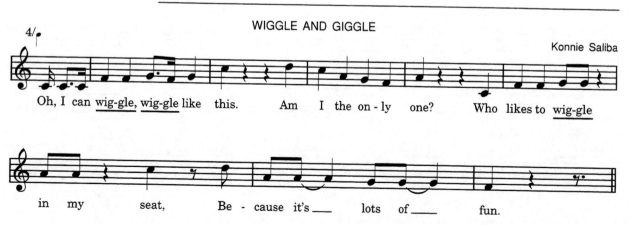

Oh, I can wig-gle, wig-gle like this. Am I the on - ly one? Who likes to wig-gle

in my seat, Be - cause it's ___ lots of ___ fun.

ACCOMPANIMENT
Alto Metallophone

Bass Xylophone

Tambourine

Verse 2. Oh I can <u>giggle</u>, <u>giggle</u> like this.
And I can't tell you why.
It's just that <u>giggling</u> feels so good,
I do it 'til I cry.

Between verses, add an interlude for speech and those playing soprano xylophones, using any notes in F pentatonic (B's and E's removed) and using the following rhythm.

Wig - gle,   Wig - gle,   Wig - gle, Wig - gle, Wig - gle.

Wig - gle, Wig - gle, Wig - gle, Wig - gle   Wig - gle.

During verses, the underlined word "wiggle" may be played by those children playing soprano xylophones; the underlined word "giggle" may be played by those playing glockenspiels (in F pentatonic).

RONDOS

Unpitched Percussion Instruments, Using Speech

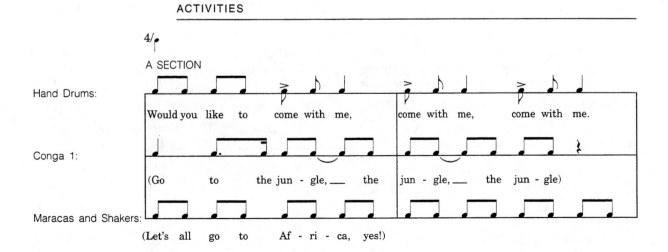

4/

A SECTION

Hand Drums:

Would you like to   come with me,   come with me,   come with me.

Conga 1:

(Go   to   the jun - gle, ___ the   jun - gle, ___ the jun - gle)

Maracas and Shakers:

(Let's all   go   to   Af - ri - ca, yes!)

Bongos:

El - el - el - e-phant, the el - e-phant.

Clapping:

Make word visuals for all parts in the A, B, and C sections. Teach the entire rondo with words and body percussion before transferring to unpitched percussion instruments.

The C Section begins with the temple blocks. The child playing the temple blocks performs the part 8 times. After 2 performances on the temple blocks, the child playing the cow bells enters and performs that part 6 times. After 2 performances, the child playing the bongos enters and performs 4 times. After 2 performances, the children who are to clap enter and perform 2 times.

Suggestion for form: Perform the entire rondo without words. Add the B and C sections to the last A Section.

Barred Instruments

ACTIVITIES
_____

RONDO

Konnie Saliba

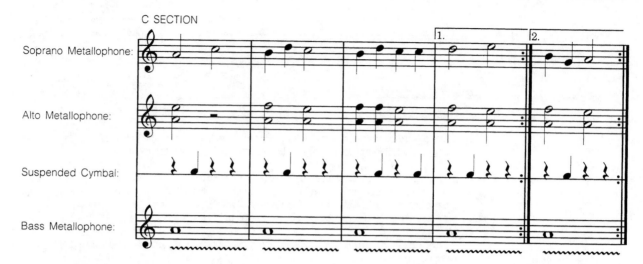

Consider creating words for each melody, or make melodic visuals for each. If you use words after the children have learned the melody, have them sing the melody using letter names. If you use a melodic visual, have the children sing letter names before playing the melody on instruments.

Play as an ABACA rondo; as a French rondo (ABACABA).

INSTRUMENTAL CANONS

Canon in Four Parts

ACTIVITIES

Make a visual of each of the four phrases of the canon. Have the children sing each phrase using letter names. Have them play each, using fingernails, then mallets. Divide into the four families and have the children play as a four-part instrumental canon, beginning with soprano instruments and adding alto instruments, glockenspiels, and bass instruments.

Canon in Two Parts for Hand Drums

ACTIVITIES

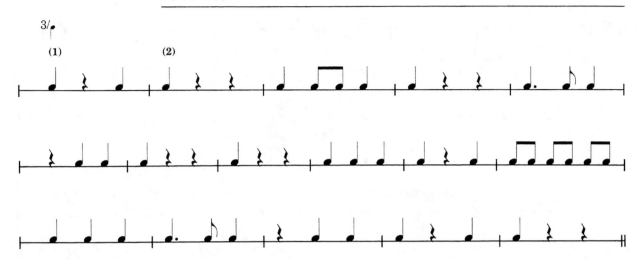

Have the children read the rhythm aloud, from notation. Then let them clap the rhythm before playing it on hand drums. Memorize. Divide the class into two groups and play in two parts, one measure apart.

Additional activity: Develop floor patterns and movement for the rhythm.

COMPOSITIONS FOR SPECIFIC GROUPS OF INSTRUMENTS

Unpitched Percussion: Woods

Wood instruments have a dry sound and can be used for fast, rhythmic compositions.

ACTIVITIES

*Use three, if possible, playing above rhythm on random pitches.

Have the children read the rhythms from notation. Have them clap each rhythm several times or until it is secure before transferring to unpitched percussion instruments. Begin the ostinati patterns with the timpani and then add rhythms from the wood block downward.

Unpitched Percussion: Metals

Metal instruments have a ringing, quiet, mysterious, calm sound and can be used for rhythms that are not too fast.

ACTIVITIES

I WISH I COULD FLY

OSTINATO

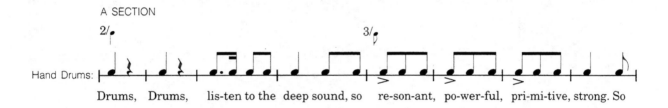

Bell Tree:	
Sleigh Bells:	
Suspended Cymbal:	
Gong:	

Teach the rhythm with words before transferring to triangle. Add the ostinato accompaniment.

Unpitched Percussion: Drums

ACTIVITIES

A SECTION

Hand Drums:

Drums,   Drums,   lis-ten to the deep sound, so   re-son-ant, po-wer-ful, pri-mi-tive, strong. So

re-son-ant,   po-wer-ful,   pri-mi-tive, strong.

B SECTION

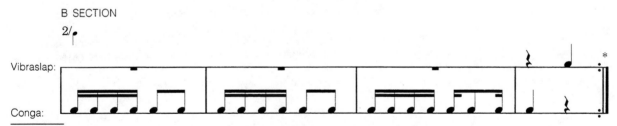

Vibraslap:

Conga:

*On the repeat of the B Section, add bongos or other drum sounds or both.

Teach the A Section with words before transferring to hand drums. The B Section can be learned by rote, patting the knees. The class can experience a gradual crescendo by repeating the entire form three or four times and, with each repeat, adding other drum sounds.

Glockenspiels

The sound of the glockenspiel is bright, childlike, and magic.

ACTIVITIES

BUTTERCUPS AND DAISIES

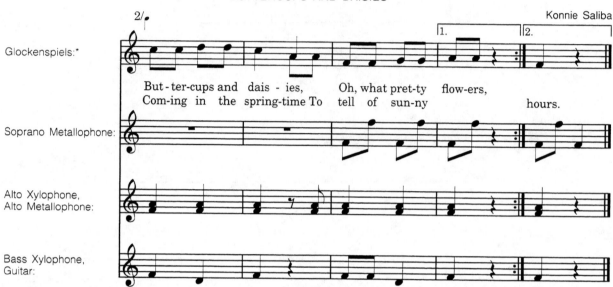

Konnie Saliba

Glockenspiels:*

But - ter-cups and dais - ies,   Oh, what pret-ty   flow-ers,
Com-ing in   the spring-time To   tell   of   sun-ny

                                                                    hours.

Soprano Metallophone:

Alto Xylophone,
Alto Metallophone:

Bass Xylophone,
Guitar:

*Glockenspiels play the melody on the repeat.

Have the children sing the 8-measure melody; repeat without singing, asking those playing glockenspiels to play the melody. Have the glockenspiels in F pentatonic (B's and E's removed) create a B Section of improvisation for the length of the A Section.

Movement:

A Section: Circle formation, hands held. Ask those moving to move into the center for four measures, raising hands upward, and out for four measures, lowering hands. Repeat the movement.

B Section: While the glockenspiels improvise, ask those moving to internalize the words and move freely and expressively in the space, returning to the circle formation for a repeat of the A Section.

Metallophones

The sound of the metallophone is rich, hazy, and mysterious.

ACTIVITIES

POETRY AND SOUND

Poem: "Good Night, Good Night"[5]

The dark is dreaming.
Day is done.
Good night, good night
To everyone.

Good night to the birds.
And the fish in the sea.
Good night to the bears
And good night to me.

Have the children play "Poetry and Sound" once. On the repeat, add "Good Night Good Night"
spoken, expressively, by a soloist or a small group.

Xylophones

The sound of the xylophone is dry, forceful, and exciting.

XYLOPHONE MADNESS

Konnie Saliba

*Observe the fermata after the repeat.

B SECTION: Speech

Hey, Ya, Hey, Ya, Hey, Ya, Hey, Ya, Hey, Ya, Hey, Ya, Hey, Ya, Hey, Ya,

Hey, Ya, Hey, Ya, Hey, Ya, Hey, Ya, Hey, Ya, Hey, Ya, Ho!

Movement:

A Section: Circle formation, moving counterclockwise, hands free
Measures 1–2: Leaps, eight in all, beginning on the right foot

[5]"Good Night, Good Night" by Dennis Lee from *Jelly Belly* by Dennis Lee, published by Macmillan of Canada © 1983, Dennis Lee.

Measure 3: Four walking steps

Measure 4: Facing center, step right, left, right in place

Repeat A Section, moving clockwise.

B Section: Speech, accompanied by

Clap:

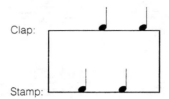

Stamp:

Measures 1–4: Moving into center, forward

Measures 5–8: Moving out from center, backward

VOICES AND INSTRUMENTS

The sound of voices and Orff instruments is exciting, particularly when the melody is sung in canon.

ACTIVITIES

GLORIA

Konnie Saliba

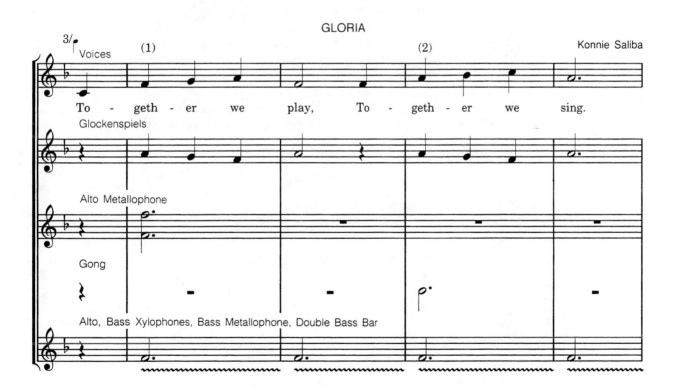

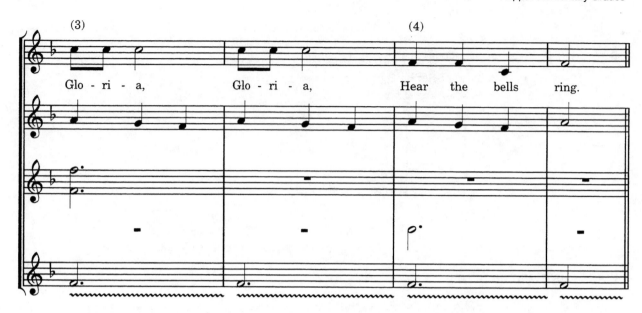

Even though the melody is in F major, put all instruments in F pentatonic (B's and E's removed) so that group improvisation is possible. After the children have learned the melody, divide the group into four sections and have them sing the melody in canon.

Suggestion for extending the form:

A: Sing the melody in unison, with accompaniment.

B: All metallophones improvise in cluster sounds for the length of the melody.

A: Sing in unison, with accompaniment.

C: All xylophones improvise for the length of the melody.

A: Sing in unison, with accompaniment.

D: All glockenspiels improvise for the length of the melody.

A: Sing the melody in four-part canon, stopping with the conductor on a chord sound.

Appendix

RANGES OF INSTRUMENTS

Range of the Barred Instruments

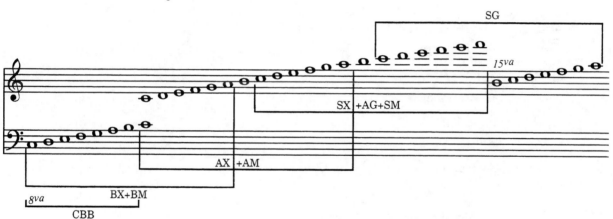

All bar instruments are notated: actual notated pitch.) (Only AX and AM sound

Range of the Recorders

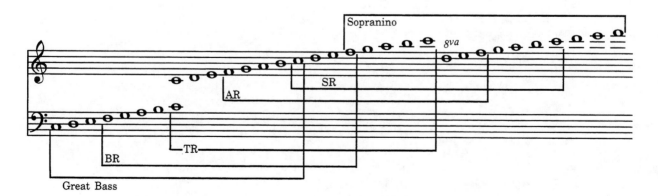

INSTRUMENTAL ORDER

This chart gives the order of instruments on a score, with abbreviations and symbols.

S	Voice:	Soprano
A		Alto
T		Tenor
B		Bass
SoR	Sopranino Recorder	
SR	Soprano Recorder	
AR	Alto Recorder	
TR	Tenor Recorder	
BR	Bass Recorder	

SG	Soprano Glockenspiel
AG	Alto Glockenspiel
glks	Both Glockenspiels
SX	Soprano Xylophone
AX	Alto Xylophone
SM	Soprano Metallophone
AM	Alto Metallophone
BX	Bass Xylophone
BM	Bass Metallophone
CBB	Contra Bass Bar
	Guitar
	Timpani
P	Piano
	Hard Mallets

Metals

- Triangle
- Finger Cymbals
- Jingle Clog
- Jingle Bells
- Bell Tree
- Cow Bell
- Agogo Bells

Woods

- Claves
- Wood Block
- Two-tone Woodblock
- Castanets
- Maracas
- Cabaza
- Rattles
- Temple Blocks
- Vibra Slap
- Guiro
- Log Drum
- Sand Blocks

Membranes

- Hand Drums
- Tambourine
- Bongo
- Conga
- Snare Drum

Big Percussion

- Hanging Cymbal
- Gong
- Bass Drum
- Cymbals

HAND SIGNAL CHART

Revised Curwen Signals

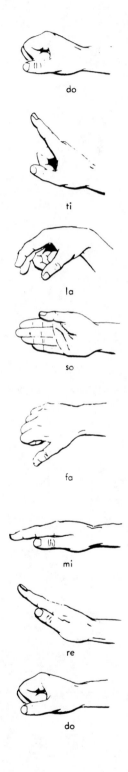

do

ti

la

so

fa

mi

re

do

Index of Songs

Index of Poems